P9-DNJ-182

THE STATES:
UNITED THEY FELL

Continued from front flap

Though business is not immune to the old political "grab," the public is the usual and uncomplaining victim. In this connection, the author brings to center stage the "true constituency," the traditional vested interests, from banking to trucking, from gas and oil to electric power. He cannot resist having fun and games with the lobbyists, those smoothly operating representatives of the true constituency, and he records both the varieties of payoffs and the methods of making them.

Finally, Mr. Trippett speculates on the future of the states and suggests that the state legislatures will endure, if only for sentimental reasons. If not for that, he goes on, then surely for laughs.

Frank Trippett is an associate editor in the National Affairs Department of *Newsweek* magazine, specializing in writing on government and politics. Before joining *Newsweek* he was capital bureau chief for the St. Petersburg, Florida, *Times,* for which he reported and commented on the State Legislature and on government in other areas of the South. Mr. Trippett has twice received the National Headline Award for political writing, and he is the recipient of a special citation from the American Political Science Association for his writing on state and local governments.

The STATES: UNITED they fell

THE
STATES:
UNITED
THEY FELL
Frank Trippett

THE WORLD PUBLISHING COMPANY • CLEVELAND AND NEW YORK

Thanks are due the following for permission to reprint passages from the works indicated:

Little, Brown and Company: From *Witch Hunt* by Carey McWilliams. Copyright 1950 by Carey McWilliams. Reprinted by permission of Little, Brown and Company.

Mr. Willie Morris: From "Legislating in Texas," which appeared in *Commentary*, November 1964.

W. W. Norton & Company, Inc.: From *The American Constitution— Its Origins and Development* by Alfred H. Kelly and Winfred A. Harbison. Copyright 1948 and 1955 by W. W. Norton & Company, Inc.; Copyright © 1963 by W. W. Norton & Company, Inc. Reprinted by permission of W. W. Norton & Company, Inc.

Henry Regnery Company: From *The Sovereign States* by James Jackson Kilpatrick. Copyright © 1957 by James Jackson Kilpatrick. Reprinted by permission of Henry Regnery Company.

Robert G. Sherrill: From "Florida's Legislature," which appeared in *Harper's*, November 1965.

The quotations from "End of Road in Sight for the States?" appeared in a copyrighted article in *U.S. News & World Report*, March 29, 1965.

Published by The World Publishing Company
2231 West 110th Street, Cleveland, Ohio 44102

Published simultaneously in Canada by Nelson, Foster & Scott Ltd.

First Printing 1967

Copyright © 1967 by Frank Trippett

All rights reserved. No part of this book may be reproduced in any form without written permission from the publisher, except for brief passages included in a review appearing in a newspaper or magazine.

Library of Congress Catalog Card Number: 66–25891

Printed in the United States of America

The STATES: UNITED they fell

328.73
T737s

97245

*"The truth is
that the State has
shrivelled up."*

—Bryce

AUTHOR'S FORENOTE

The purpose of the following notes and comments is not
to prove that the state has
shrivelled up but to suggest
how and why.

F. T.
Larchmont, New York
April 27, 1966

1

"EVERYTHING IN THE NA-
TURE OF STATE POLICY BE-
LONGS TO THE LEGISLATURE,
AND TO THE LEGISLATURE
ALONE."

—Bryce

★★★★★★★★★★★★★★★★★★★★
★★★★★★★★★★★★★★★★★★★★

In almost every important way the American states are in some dubious condition. For the most part the U.S. citizenry could scarcely care less. "The American people," V. O. Key put it more tenderly, "are not boiling with concern about the workings of their state governments."

This popular indifference is well documented. It is a source of much anxiety to students of government. Many are tempted to blame this indifference for the plight of the states. "I am convinced," says Jefferson B. Fordham, dean of the Pennsylvania University Law School, "that they are relatively weak and underdeveloped governmental organs because we have not had the interest nor will to make them anything else." Public apathy is thus construed as the cause of the sorry performance of the states. It results in low-quality legislatures, hence mediocre performance.

I take exception to this and suggest that instead the popular attitude is one result of the way the states have performed. Public indifference is primarily evidence that the states possess only limited relevancy to American society. It did not cause the organic atrophy that obtains in state government. Rather, it is the understandable response of a society that long since has come to expect little from the states. Massive and enduring public indifference is but one conspicuous sign that the states have fallen low indeed in the American scheme of things.

Though the states exhibit precious little vitality and the people precious little concern, it is nevertheless worthwhile to understand just how the states have fallen, how far, how finally. It is important if only to help dispel the wistful hopes for state action that perennially befog political debates over national objectives. Congress receives few major domestic proposals that are not confused or impeded by complaints that they intrude into fields where the states alone should act. But is there any longer a legitimate hope that the states will take a substantial part in shaping a better society?

One glaring truth of the times is that most of the perplexing domestic problems confronting the country today would not exist if the states had acted. But they possessed neither the vision, the will, the vitality, the imagination nor the determination to act. Indisputably, the states possessed the power to act—and the duty. Yet, a festering complex of problems—ranging from crowded slums to overcrowded schools, from crowded prisons to overcrowded mental hospitals—stand as testimony to insufficient action, power unused, duty neglected. The present era has confronted a long and agonizing conflict over civil rights only because of historic state failure.

To speak of the states in this regard is not to speak of their terrain or their populations or the arbitrary boundaries that squiggle and slice across maps of the continent. It is certainly not to speak of the states as though they were the sentimental abstractions conjured up in popular ballads, misty anthems and collegiate marching songs. It is not even to speak of state governments as such; these, as administrative and judicial instruments, perform tolerably well much of the time.

To diagnose the states as organs of government is to diagnose the state legislatures. ". . . We are led back to the legislature," said Bryce seventy-five years ago. ". . . We may almost call it the government and ignore all other authorities." This is true today and was at the Republic's beginning. Anyone writing of the state as an instrument of government must write of the legislature. To indict the states is to indict the legislatures.

They have, of course, been well indicted many times during the last century and a half—so frequently, I suspect, that many of us think of them only in a habitual way. This is to suggest that we commonly do not think about the legislatures at all. Instead, we merely tend to recollect what has been demonstrated so often: that legislatures are inefficient and corrupt, that they procrastinate on public business while habitually kowtowing to private economic interests, that legislators get drunk and disorderly and consort with ladies procured by avaricious lobbyists, that they line their own pockets, scratch their own backs and roll their own logs—all the while stamping out progressive legislation in the name of protecting their constituents.

We tend further to recall that legislatures chronically disobey their own state constitutions. "For years," said Adlai Stevenson, while governor of Illinois, "the machinery of our state government has been kept in motion only by continued violations of plain and positive provisions in the Illinois constitution. . . . When we lose respect for constitutional government, we lose respect for democracy."

Legislatures also, we recall, complain incessantly about how little money they make, and they squabble compulsively and obsessively and ceaselessly over trivia that has no more impact on the fate of the world than the breath of a gnat. I have searched for a word to describe the state legislatures' obsessive-compulsive attention to microscopically trivial detail. Finding none, I have invented one. The disease is *microphilia*. Perhaps the word will be useful to doctors who find themselves treating patients who compulsively look for fly specks in the pepper.

We naturally tend to recall that state legislatures display a deathless penchant for buffoonery. It is hard to forget.

It is all true, too. But what is one to make of it? How is one to account for the peculiar characteristics of state legislatures? Why do they leave so much undone while doing so

much that seems hardly worth doing? So much that simply
should not be done?

There is no shortage of information about legislatures.
Scholars and journalists have examined their performance,
their work habits, their staff personnel, their various political appurtenances and forms. A considerable body of theory, criticism and analysis exists. Despite this, there has
been surprisingly little reflection and speculation on *why*
state legislatures behave as they do. Professional observers
investigate the nature of the states or state politics or state
government or state-federal relations within the constrictions of fairly consistent predilections.

Politicians, though pragmatists almost to a man, tend
to analyze conditions in terms of windy theory and doctrine
that conceals far more than it reveals.

Journalists instinctively stick close to the spectacular
and scandalous and sensational in legislative activity. They
have little incentive to probe the deeper institutional anatomy. Newspaper publishers, after all, generally share the
public indifference to state government and prove it by al-
lotting mere driblets of space to news in this field.

Political scientists have unearthed ponderous masses of
lore about state legislatures. Yet, these academicians remain
enamoured of methodology to a degree that seriously shack-
les them even while lending their findings a faint scientific
aroma. Too often the political scientist seems bent on proving (and proving and proving) the failure of the statistical
method as an instrument for fathoming politics. They do not
jump to conclusions and often seem reluctant to reach them
at all.

Historians stick close to the significant roles that state
legislatures have played in events. This is helpful, but not
too. After all, the state legislatures' preoccupation with the
insignificant—their chronic microphilia—must be viewed as
one of their most significant characteristics.

For all these limitations, however, politicians, journalists, political scientists and historians have provided an extensive picture of state legislatures. It is a fairly astonishing

picture, showing a political organism that is variously comical and exasperating and repellent, now and then heartening and finally baffling and provoking. An observer is impelled to wonder that the lawmaking bodies of the American states arrived at the condition in which we find them.

The purpose of these notes and comments is not only to spotlight the condition of the states but also to suggest new ways of understanding why they are thus. This book is an attempt to illuminate certain idiomorphic traits and impulses that are to be found in the state legislatures. I shall amply describe what one scholar, Charles Warren in his history of the Supreme Court, called "the sly and stealthy arts to which state legislatures are exposed." At the same time I shall attempt to comprehend why, as one New Jersey governor, A. Harry Moore, once put it, "An 'indissoluble union of indestructible states' is rapidly becoming an indissoluble union of impotent states." Moore himself was half-quoting Supreme Court Justice Chase's famed comment. It was another New Jersey governor, Charles Edison, son of Thomas Alva, who said that "state government is the most antiquated, incompetent part of our whole American system." My view will not contradict his.

In the course of these notes I shall suggest how the conventional lore, theory and doctrine about the states tend to camouflage the actuality of state legislative behavior. This is not to confess an iconoclastic obsession. Doctrine and theory are not necessarily disagreeable. Occasionally they even advance understanding. But often they do not.

As an example, the doctrine of states' rights is one of the greatest hoaxes ever perpetrated upon the common folk. It is to be compared with the slogans invoked by Urban II, Peter the Hermit and the legislatures of the medieval church (as the diocesan councils functioned) to shoo all their sorefooted flocks off to the Crusades. *Peccaminum remissio* indeed. (The crusades for states' rights have been comparably fruitful, too. While the Crusades sought to extend Christendom to the East, they ended with the Mohammedan East advancing deep into the West, the recession of Christianity in the East after the thirteenth century being one of history's more striking developments.) Doctrine, in any event, is not so often descriptive as propagandistic.

Throughout this endeavor I shall draw partly upon extensive reading in the field, partly upon the firsthand experience of my years of observing legislatures and politics as a reporter and writer. In general, of course, personal observation only vividly confirms the sometimes unsettling picture of legislative behavior that has been conveyed in print. After long scrutiny of a single legislature one can accept as credible the stories of how New York's was literally auctioned off in a financial battle between two great corporate barons, how Indiana's lawmakers once established a standard scale of bribes, how the Montana legislature functioned as a chamber of abject stooges for a single mining company. After personal experience one can better understand current journalism (how the Massachusetts Crime Commission could denounce the General Court for moral spinelessness) and more comfortably digest history. It becomes easier to envision how Louisiana's legislators were bought and sold like "sacks of potatoes" (as Huey Long boasted), how Georgia's were bribed almost to the last man in one of the nation's great land-sale scandals. One no longer imagines that cynicism lay behind FDR's twinkling accounting, in private to a White House correspondent, of how much bribe money would be needed to kill a constitutional amendment in the state legislatures. One no longer boggles incredulously over the accounts of the opening of the Arkansas legislature when the speaker stabbed a contentious member to death, and of the time in the Illinois House when State Representative Abraham Lincoln leaped out of a window to thwart an attempt to muster a quorum. To witness a legislature for years is finally to believe legislatures capable of anything. As one state representative once put it to me about his colleagues: "Sometimes they're near thandal [*sic*]."

Beyond this, actually witnessing the marvelous world of the state legislature is perhaps the surest way to discover the actuality that does sometimes contrast sharply with what is written and said on the subject. One is prompted to doubt some important parts of the conventional lore. The chronic condition of fiscal crisis in the states, for instance, appears to be more a product of legislative rhetoric than of economic fact. And those interminable legislative battles over reapportionment are not always what they appear to be. There will be more about all of this, of course.

At the outset, however, I ought to acknowledge some of the things that I do not purport to be doing. This is certainly not an effort to write history, though my views naturally spring from my own reading of history, pertinent fragments of which are stitched herein. This is not an attempt to Guntherize the states or the state governments. Nor is it an attempt to produce a textbook, a guidebook, a reference book or an academic tome. Finally, this is not a pleading. It is not to urge that the states be strengthened. It is not to urge that they be done away with.

My observation is that history has long since determined the place of the states in the American scheme and that place is not likely to change substantially. I do recommend that we try to understand it. Thus the modest object of these notes and comments: I wish primarily to develop some observations that may alleviate some of the bafflement that state legislatures so regularly produce.

2

★★★★★★★★★★★★★★★★★★★★★
★★★★★★★★★★★★★★★★★★★★★

"THE METAMORPHOSIS OF
THE STATE LEGISLATURES
CONSTITUTES AN ODD CHAP-
TER IN THE HISTORY OF
POPULAR GOVERNMENT. AT
ONE TIME REGARDED AS THE
SYMBOLIC EMBODIMENT OF
THE PEOPLE ASSEMBLED,
THE STATE LEGISLATURE
WENT INTO A LONG DE-
CLINE."

—Key

★★★★★★★★★★★★★★★★★★★★★
★★★★★★★★★★★★★★★★★★★★★

To hear some liberals tell it,
the states are sick to the death. And good riddance.

On the other flank, deep-dyed conservatives warn that
if the states are going to hell the federal government is
sending them there. And too bad.

Such roughly are the two primary schools of theory,
criticism, doctrine, ideology and speculation.

One school focuses on the institutional failings of the
states—failures in function, in character. State deficiencies
generally are viewed as organic and usually self-imposed.

Though the other, the conservative school, sometimes
acknowledges the existence of the states' shortcomings, its
overriding view is that the states are victims of external
forces—weak because the federal government has grabbed
strength away from them. The word "grab," used just so,
recurs like a drumbeat in this conservative school of comment. Its adherents tend to indulge the conspiratorial theory
of history.

One quality at least appears consistently in comment
about the plight of the states: the rhetoric of crisis prevails,
the language is sharp with a foresmell of doom.

"The shadow of State government may long be retained when the substance is totally lost and forgotten." This foreboding rumble comes from a politically powerful Pennsylvanian. It does not matter that he spoke before the union was founded, an apprehensive antifederalist named Smilie. His style endures.

It thrives, in fact, in that apprehensive antifederalist pamphlet, *U.S. News & World Report.* From the issue of March 29, 1965, comes the following headline that preceded a five-page essay:

END OF ROAD IN SIGHT
FOR THE STATES?

It's a hastening trend: Power, more and more, is shifting away from the 50 state capitals and concentrating in Washington.

Latest move in that direction: A White House bid for power to police registration and voting in at least six states of the South.

The shift already has gone a long way.

Washington lays down standards for hiring in private business. Wages and hours are regulated. Discrimination is barred in hotels, restaurants. Farmers are told what they can plant.

The gradual surrender of the states to federal authority has been accelerating since the start of the "New Deal."

That "headline" encapsulates the orthodox archconservative view. The "story" that followed did not substantially modify it.

For some reason the contrary liberal extreme—that the states are dying and should—does not often appear under the sponsorship of a prosperous mass magazine. It has found its way into *The Nation,* however. Here from the issue of November 16, 1963, is its gist as expressed by a professor and editor named Jerome Ellison:

"Our state legislatures," he begins with a familiar note, "are the least competent and most corrupt of all our constituted political bodies." He goes on to raise grave questions about the literacy of the legislators, questions their magnanimity ("the pettiest"), strongly suggesting that their probity is not what it might be ("the most readily bribed of all public officials"). And on, to state that even the boundaries of the states lack logic, that under state government municipalities and subdivisions have proliferated to hamstring and harass each other, that the political obsolescence matches the geographic obsolescence, that the states can neither legislate well nor administer well ("They have rarely been able to carry through administrative jobs more complicated than mailing out license plates"), and he concludes: ". . . In many aspects state government is dead, and ripe for burying."

These two sample views, from Ellison and *U.S. News,* share something in common besides alarmed language. Each advances a grim prognosis for the states. The one regretfully divines that "the end of the road" is at hand for the states; the other gleefully fantasizes their final interment. Each nurses a pervasive suspicion that the plight of the states is worsening. Neither does much to advance understanding.

By the conservative plaint, resting on the belief that the states are being victimized by the federal government, one is invited to be frightened by some metaphysical horrorland in which a power-hungry goblin called Washington is cunningly sucking its fill from reservoirs of political power that lie out there in the states. Conservative metaphors describing the federal monster change form but not intent. Invariably, insatiable Washington is snatching or grabbing something away from the states. Finally, the pitch only diverts the observer from regarding the blighted anatomy of the states.

The liberal antistate view disconcerts in a different way. It beguiles one with its appealing belief that political affairs might be more orderly, more neatly arranged, more logically structured, more nicely tuned. State boundaries do not appear to have been rationally laid out, so let's. Et cetera. The view presupposes possibilities of reasonable-

itself in a variety of other observable symptoms: political alienation, social irresponsibility, moral corruption, atrophied imagination, incompetence in self-management and a susceptibility to paranoia. Where but in the Georgia legislature would one lone pacifistic Negro representative have been kicked out on the ground that he was a menace to the Republic? Where? In New York, where the legislature once denied seats to five Socialists on a comparable ground. This and kindred behavior will be noted in detail later.

For the moment I only want to suggest roughly the method of observation that will be employed in the pages that follow. Malapportionment will be taken as just one more sign of some deeper character that seems to determine state legislative behavior regardless of time and place. Other pronounced legislative dispositions will be so taken, too, and I shall attempt to discover the relationships between them. The historic resistance to fair apportionment, for instance, seems closely related to the legislature's historic subservience to the commercial community, which in turn is intimately related to the legislative aversion to fair taxation and the persistent neglect of public projects. The legislature's chronic microphilia, that obsession with trivia, may be a rather direct result of the fact that its main creative force has been consistently thwarted by its other traits and dispositions. Such hypotheses, in any event, are worth weighing.

The notes, comments and speculations that follow are concerned with the political and social vitality of the state legislature, with its morality and attitudes, with the stance in which it has usually been found in the development of this society.

Before pushing on, however, I offer glimpses of some curious things that can be seen and heard at legislature time under those state capitol domes across the land.

3

★★★★★★★★★★★★★★★★★★★★
★★★★★★★★★★★★★★★★★★★★

"CYNICS CLAIM THIS LEGIS-
LATURE WILL BE DISTIN-
GUISHED BY ITS HAVING
NAMED A STATE DOG AND
PAYING AT LEAST CURSORY
ATTENTION TO SELECTION
OF A STATE FISH. THE
PEOPLE HAVE A RIGHT TO
MORE."
—*The Philadelphia Evening
Bulletin,* on Pennsylvania's
1965 session

★★★★★★★★★★★★★★★★★★★★
★★★★★★★★★★★★★★★★★★★★

In action the American state
legislature is incomparable. But it has been frequently compared—to a bawdy house, a country fair, a camp meeting,
a service club social, a circus of follies and a carnival of
tumblebugs, each rolling up his own pile.

Perhaps these are exaggerations. Still, in any state capitol when the legislature comes to town, even the untrained
eye can detect the embryo of each hyperbole.

A session usually pops, crackles and sloshes in the
raunchy, raucous, back-slapping aura of a Shriners' convention. It is charged with the hyperkinetic conviviality of a
fraternity reunion amidst the woolly earnestness of a
League of Women Voters chapter trying to get organized.

On opening day many chambers are banked with gi-
gantic gaudy floral offerings, a luxuriant, multicolored visual
assault that makes the viewer think it would be appropriate
if a gangster were about to be buried. The cadences of habitual and predictable oratory gush up in the air over
shuffling fumbling rote-stiff ceremonials: members commonly go through the ritualistic charade of electing all over

again speakers already designated. Newly elected lawmakers, shiny greenlings, step forward to be sworn; they glow radiantly like Girl Scouts picking up blue ribbons for selling the most cookies.

From Little Rock to Olympia, from Austin to Montpelier, the legislature is a sight to behold. After the thing has got going the chamber is a cacophonous vista of milling and huddling, paper-shuffling and sandwich-munching and the restless fidgetings of the makers of law behind opened newspapers in the morning. Here is the crude and murmurous ballet of legislative routine, a seemingly ceaseless scene played to the cryptic and almost indecipherable chant of bill clerks reading fragments of bill titles: cues to the semaphoric nods and handwaves from the floor or chair that sends legislation on its way. Law is fashioned with more casualness than pigs are bought at a crossroads auction. The routine intrigues the spectator sheerly by its appearance of ceaseless and directionless motion, and by its sounds: the rhythm is that of babbling brook and roaring surf. "Take up the next bill! Take up the next bill!" It is all more hypnotic than exciting. Yet, such is the whimsical temper of state legislators that there is ever a chance one will witness one of those moments for which they are much too well known.

It is too late, alas, to see Arkansas House Speaker John Wilson descend from the rostrum, draw his bowie knife and advance toward State Representative Joseph J. Anthony, also armed with a knife. Someone threw a chair between them, Anthony dropped his knife and Wilson sank his in Anthony's chest, killing him instantly. This was in December 1837. The Arkansas House was discussing a bill aimed at the extermination of wolves. The problem was to identify and certify the remains of wolves on which bounties should be paid. It was Anthony's fate to offer an amendment to the bill providing that "the signature of the President of the Real Estate Bank should be attached to the certificate of the wolf scalp." This failed to amuse Speaker Wilson, who also happened to be the president of the Real Estate Bank of Arkansas, a recent creation of the brand-new legislature.

Wilson asked Anthony if he intended anything personal. When Anthony replied that he did not, Wilson asked him to sit down. Anthony insisted on explaining his amendment. "Sit down, or I'll make you," Wilson shouted. He did, of course. Though he was expelled as speaker for the impropriety, Wilson was subsequently acquitted of a murder indictment, after which he rose in open court and ordered the sheriff to "take the jury to a dram-shop." Wilson, jury and friends paraded through the streets until daylight making a great and joyous din on drums, trumpets and tin pans. It is too late, alas, to see it.

It is also too late, of course, to see Abraham Lincoln leap out the window of the statehouse at Springfield. This was in 1840 at the height of a contentious wrangle over a banking bill. There came a call for a quorum, a parliamentary move by the Democrats to skin the Whig side. Suddenly, as the clerk began to sound the roll, the tall, gangling young Whig leaped from his seat. He loped to the window, quickly swung it open and—in a blur of knobby knees and feet and elbows—leaped to the ground below. The quorum was had nonetheless. And the Democratic bill was voted on and passed. But it was only later that the news of this got to Lincoln, who had landed unhurt in the muddy snow one floor below. By the next day there were half-earnest proposals for raising the statehouse a floor to thwart such strategy in the future—and in the 1870s, when a new capitol was built with a statue of Lincoln at the entrance, the legislative chambers were in fact lodged on the third floor. No one since has emulated Lincoln's leap. Still, there have been sights to see in our own era and even in Illinois.

In the 1965 session at Springfield, State Representative Joseph P. Stremlau caught his colleagues' attention by brandishing a pistol and cranking a shrill siren—the seventy-two-year-old retired farmer's way of dramatizing his opposition to a bill that would abolish capital punishment. "How many people are alive today because of the death penalty?" demanded Stremlau, picking up a .32-caliber revolver and waving it as he began sounding a small police siren on his desk. A veteran of eighteen years in the

House, Stremlau left the question tactfully unanswered. He did, however, claim that when he was a deputy sheriff in 1935 a bank robber had poked that very pistol in his belly. "Why didn't he pull the trigger?" thundered Stremlau. Here came an answer: "Because he knew if he did—he'd *fry!*"

The state legislature is a feast of improbable sights, improbable utterances, improbable proposals, improbable actions.

Maryland's famed lawmakers reassembled in the capitol in Annapolis after joyous rounds of St. Patrick's Day parties in 1965, and as they reeled to their seats it seemed possible that some remained ambulatory only on a point of personal privilege. The chamber bubbled over with the hubbub of a neighborhood tavern. Two members began cleaning off their desks—by wadding up the papers and throwing them at each other, then at their colleagues. A few lawmakers still wore silly green pasteboard hats that abound on such festive Irish days. Every call for order only raised a thick-tongued chorus of demands for adjournment *sine die*. Though the calendar was loaded, Speaker Marvin Mandel (successor to an ex-speaker who was absent, completing a prison term for fraud) decided that his wards were more so. He dissolved the session with an immortal ruling: "We can't go on like this!"

Such was the high point of a wild, unproductive, seventy-day session that was finally terminated on the day that the Maryland Senate speedily *passed* a bill about which Senate President William S. James asked, *without* getting an answer: "Does anyone here know what this bill is all about?"

Legislatures do go on like that—not always gassed, to be sure, but with magnificent abandon.

In Georgia at the close of a recent session Representative Harry Mixon of Irwin County initiated the following exchange with Acting Speaker Clarence Vaughan.

"Mr. Speaker, would it be in order for the House to go to the Senate and hoot at 'em?"

"I think," said Vaughan, "that it would be perfectly in order."

Such, occasionally, was the quality of decorum in the capitol at Atlanta that one legislator who fell to the floor and began twitching because of an epileptic seizure received no assistance for perhaps ten minutes. No one was sure that anything was wrong. Georgia Representative Grover Lee once demonstrated the call of a train conductor on the floor—a challenge that Representatives Howard Rainey and Ben Jessup accepted by impersonating automobile auctioneers. It was all in the spirit of the time that Representative Dewey Rush of Tattnall County interrupted proceedings on a point of personal privilege to sing a song ("I've Been Hanging Around This Old Town Too Long")— all of which more or less explains why Representative George Bagby of Paulding County once also broke into the formalities to say: "Mr. Speaker, I don't know what's going on. There's too much confusion in and around the tabernacle."

Onward:

In Ohio, one lawmaker entered a debate over an existing law to propound the year's most perplexing question: "Mr. Speaker, if it's in the law now, how can we change it?" And in Florida, State Representative George Hollahan, a lawyer, lofted a speech in behalf of a censorship bill right up to this totally solemn and serious declaration: "Freedom of speech is a *privilege*, not a *right*!" Now there was a proposition that might well have surprised those revered shades that Florida Senator Charley Johns has occasionally called "Our Foundling Fathers."

Each legislature has its moments. In California, the late Senator Samuel R. Geddes used to offer almost annually a bill to require exhibitors at the annual state fair to array their cows with the heads instead of the behinds presented to audiences. An assemblyman from Redondo Beach just as persistently used to push a measure to require pay-toilet proprietors to provide a free facility for each two available for rent. And another assemblyman, proposing automatic expulsion for any state college student arrested for demonstrating, was asked whether the student should not first be given a trial. "Don't you bother me with any of your goddamned technicalities," said he.

Down in Texas, gruff and salty Senator George Parkhouse of Dallas tried to amend a barber-regulation bill to prohibit a barber from discussing "atomic or nuclear energy . . . or any other subject in which he is not learned." The amendment failed in committee. But another funny measure, a bill by State Senator Frank Owen III of El Paso to prohibit the display of the UN flag on state property, passed the senate to perish later on a narrow house vote.

Even in the bud of their statehood Alaska and Hawaii have attained the American spirit. In 1966 at Juneau, Alaska's embroiled senate dispatched a sergeant-at-arms with an arrest warrant to bring in none other than a state senator who said he was leaving because he had the flu. The flu-ridden senator, Brad Phillips of Anchorage, outwrestled the senate minion and checked into the hospital. At that point the senate decided to excuse him from voting on a pending controversy. In Honolulu, Hawaii's legislature (the only one that meets in a royal hall—Iolani Palace) found opening-day speeches in 1965 drowned out by strolling musicians. It was a happenstance that brought no complaints from spectators—because, anyway, they were watching the hula girls twitching about the floor. "Ridiculous," snorted a woman tourist from the mainland. "Just ridiculous." At other times in Honolulu, State Senator Kazuhisa Abe, a Buddhist, was keeping things lively by sponsoring bills that called for the abolition of Christmas and Easter, among other Christian holidays.

These moments come to every capitol. One came to the Tennessee legislature all because some residents of the Heiskell community near Knoxville complained that they had glimpsed naked people flitting about in a nearby woodland. State Representative A. Gaines Morton, naturally, took to a helicopter to see for himself. Just as he thought: a nudist colony. "I saw," he reported, "a half dozen men or women down below without a thing on." Morton did not explain why he failed to distinguish whether they were "men or women." But he did have in mind a law to ban nudist colonies. "Now, if people want to run around nude it makes no difference to me," he said, "but it does make a difference to neighbors in that remote area."

In the House at Nashville the questioning was painfully predictable. How many times had Morton inspected the nudists? Was he giving the legislature the bare facts? "How many nudists," asked Representative Charles Galbreath, "does it take to make a colony?" Morton did not know. And neither did the legislature (whose historic neglect of reapportionment, incidentally, led to the one-man-one-vote decision). Nonetheless, it promptly passed a bill that was just as promptly challenged by the American Sunbathing Association, Inc. It was quickly invalidated as unconstitutional by two federal judges who said: "The words of the act, if literally construed, would prevent nudism in health clubs, YMCA's, school gyms or other recreational systems, and possibly at home." Next time, Morton vowed, he would draft a bill "with teeth."

In one of *its* moments of 1965 the New Jersey legislature enacted a censorship bill of such quality that during debate Senator William E. Ozzard, an opponent, insisted that police clear the chamber of children spectators. His reason: "I intend to quote from the bill." The trouble, curiously, was that the sponsors of the measure—led by Assemblywoman Mildred Barry Hughes—had described what they regarded as pornographic in such detail that some legislators thought the bill too dirty to be put into the U.S. mails. The bill was handily passed, however, and is reproduced here for both prurient and educational purposes:

ASSEMBLY, No. 768
STATE OF NEW JERSEY
INTRODUCED MAY 17, 1965
By Assemblywoman HUGHES, Assemblyman MUSTO,
Assemblywoman KORDJA, Assemblymen CURRY,

BRIGIANI, LYNCH, McGANN, MARAZITI, KEE-GAN, SEARS, Assemblywoman HIGGINS, Assembly-men DOREN, TANZMAN, HALPIN, POLICASTRO, ADDONIZIO and BURKE.

(Without Reference)

AN ACT relating to obscenity with relation to the exposure, sale, loan, gift or distribution of certain publications, photographs, films and other materials to children under 18 years of age, and supplementing Chapter 115 of Title 2A of the New Jersey Statutes.

BE IT ENACTED by the Senate and General Assembly of the State of New Jersey:

1. As used in chapter 115 of Title 2A of the New Jersey Statutes and chapter 166 of the laws of 1962, the word "obscene," with relation to the exposure, sale, loan, gift or distribution of items or materials to a child under 18 years of age, shall mean and include:

a. Portrayal in still or motion pictures or similar representation of any person or persons of the age of puberty or older, posed or presented in such a manner as to exploit lust for commercial gain and which would appeal to the lust of persons under the age of 18 years or to their curiosity as to sex or to the anatomical differences between the sexes and which shows, depicts or reveals such person or persons:

(1) with less than a fully opaque covering of his or her genitals, pubic areas or buttocks, and, if that person is a female, with less than a fully opaque covering of any portion of the breast below a point immediately above the top of the areola, or

(2) engaged in an act or acts of masturbation, homosexuality, or sexual intercourse, or in physical contact with another person's genitals, pubic areas, buttock or buttocks or the breast or breasts of a female, or

(3) in a posture or way that the viewer's attention or concentration is primarily

focused on that person's or those persons' genitals, pubic areas, buttock or buttocks, female breast or breasts, even if those portions of the anatomy are covered, or

b. Any book, "pocket book," pamphlet or magazine, phonograph record, tape or similar electronic reproduction of sound, containing details, descriptions, or narrative accounts of:

(1) the genitals in a state or condition of sexual stimulation or arousal, or

(2) acts of masturbation, or

(3) acts of homosexuality, or

(4) acts of sexual intercourse, or

(5) acts of physical contact with another person's genitals, pubic areas, buttock or buttocks or the breast or breasts of a female, which contact is made in an act of sexual stimulation, gratification or perversion, which details, descriptions or narrative accounts are written or presented in such a manner as to exploit lust for commercial gain and which would appeal to the lust of persons under the age of 18 years or to their curiosity as to sex or to the anatomical differences between the sexes and which are to be distinguished from flat and factual statements of the facts, causes, functions or purposes of the subject of the writing or presentation, such as would be found in bona fide medical or biological textbooks.

2. If any part or provision of this act or its application to any person or circumstances is for any reason adjudged invalid or unconstitutional by a court of competent jurisdiction, such judgment shall be limited in its effect to the facts involved in the controversy in which such judgment shall have been rendered and shall not affect the validity of the remainder of this act or its application to other persons and circumstances.

3. This act shall take effect immediately.

The act, however, did not take effect. It prompted protests by, among others, the New Jersey School Library Association, the New Jersey Library Association and the New Jersey Education Association. Governor Richard Hughes pointed out some disadvantages of the bill that these groups had called to his attention.

"Books such as illustrated versions of Dante's *Inferno,* the works of Chaucer, books on the fine arts and works of our leading artists such as Michelangelo and Rodin and even materials as familiar as the *National Geographic Magazine* would fall within the interdiction of Assembly Bill No. 768," Hughes said. "Similarly, whole series of books now used in our schools, which are designed to acquaint growing adolescents with the problems of sex, would fall clearly within the language of the bill . . ."

Concluding that children did not yet need to be saved from the *National Geographic,* the governor vetoed the bill on constitutional grounds.

Legislatures seldom achieve such classic absurdity at the sacrifice of common drollery. They have it both ways. As Pennsylvanians were reminded in 1965, when the legislature solemnly declared the Great Dane to be the state dog while failing to reach agreement on a state fish, few things inspire lawmakers more than animal life. Birds. Fish. Anything of the sort sets them off. Even insects.

Illinois senators locked in passionate debate in 1965 over a proposal to shoot down the cardinal as the official state bird—and elevate the purple martin instead. No one could fathom the dark motives behind all this until Springfield bars began serving purple martinis. An alternative suggestion was advanced by Senator Anthony De Tolve, an in-law of reputed crime overlord Sam (Mooney) Giancana. De Tolve said the official state bird should be the stool pigeon.

In the same year North Carolina legislators tactfully buried a resolution to designate the bedbug as the official Tarheel insect and enacted a measure protecting alligators only after turning back amendments that would have provided similar safe passage for elephants and kangaroos.

To what is much worse:
The bear
That is rare,
The goat
That's remote,
The sheep, from which year
   after year you must
      remove the coat,
The catamount
That does not amount
      to that amount,
The cow
That somehow
We, as a human minority,
      cannot allow;
And although, as one of the
      Democratic minority,
   I should, alas,
Far prefer the jackass,
I must—until a state
      animal can choose
      its own state—
Not hesitate
To vote, of course,
For the Morgan horse.

Tomfoolery in Vermont has been pleasantly bucolic in contrast, say, to Texas. Journalist Willie Morris in the November 1964 *Commentary* recalled an episode in Austin:

One night, in a bitter floor debate in the lower house, one legislator pulled the cord out of the amplifier system, another hit him from the blindside with a tackle; there was mass pushing, hitting, clawing, and exchanges about one another's wives, mistresses, and forbears. Sweethearts and wives, who were allowed on the floor with friends and secretaries, cowered near the desks. In the middle of the brawl, a barbershop quartet of legislators quickly formed at the front of the chamber and, like a dance band during a saloon fight, sang "I Had a Dream, Dear."

That's the way it is, going west. In 1965 *Topeka State Journal* writer Jim Petterson wrote a column ("Adjournment of a Kansas legislative session is a happy event—so happy, in fact, one wonders why it isn't done sooner") in which he recalled: "In the 1925 session, when I served as a page, the final night was a near riot. It began with wads of waste paper sailing half way across Representative Hall. House members soon grabbed wire wastebaskets and placed them over their heads for protection. This was sufficient for a time, but soon inkwells were whistling through the festive air. An occasional ashtray flew by. Some solons crawled beneath their tiny desks to avoid the missiles. . . ."

Columnist Petterson also recalled the time a group of Kansas legislators took a drunken colleague to Topeka State Hospital and committed him, explaining to the attendants: "He isn't dangerous. He simply has delusions of grandeur. . . . He will try to tell you he is a member of the Kansas Legislature."

Delusions of grandeur indeed.

4

"THE LITERATURE OF FED-
ERAL-STATE RELATIONSHIPS
IS REPLETE WITH MYTHS
THAT NEED TO BE DEMOL-
ISHED."

—Orville L. Freeman

★★★★★★★★★★★★★★★★★★★★★★★
★★★★★★★★★★★★★★★★★★★★★★★

There once, to be sure, was a
race that lived "under the government of reason." They
were the Houyhnhnms. Their legislature met the test of
idealism. Here was the Swiftian world.

"Every fourth year, at the vernal equinox," it was recorded, "there is a representative council of the whole nation, which meets in a plain . . . and continues about five or
six days. Here they enquire into the state and condition of
the several districts; whether they abound or be deficient in
hay or oats, or cows or Yahoos. And wherever there is any
want (which is but seldom) it is immediately supplied by
unanimous consent and contribution."

Life among the Yahoos is different. An American legislature is as far from the ideal as the Houyhnhnms were
from the real. The actuality could scarcely be more removed
from both textbook theory and the inspirational notion that
the Supreme Court rephrased in 1964.

"State legislatures," said the court, "are, historically,
the fountainhead of representative government in this country."

Underneath those state capitol domes, with their jelly-
mold similarity, the innocent encounters reality by degrees.
As the legislature convenes, the spectacle bears some resemblance to the theory one has heard. Here come the lawmakers from the several districts to attend the wants of
the people therein. For a time one retains the notion of the
people as the *constituency* of the lawmakers. Such is

the theory. The people out there somewhere have sent their elected delegates to the capitol to attend their wants— while, of course, safeguarding their treasured rights.

So here sit the representatives, there the senators. They reign in swivel chairs, usually, behind desks ordered in neat arcs across the carpeted floors of great vaulted chambers. Separate chambers, of course, reflect the theory that each branch is a check upon the foibles of the other.

Committees are established—a fragmentation, the innocent reflects, in the interest of efficiency. Proposed legislation must be refined by the mill of close reason before it is placed before the general membership for deliberation. Just so, the theory.

In a mechanical way, the spectacle follows form: House. Senate. Committees. Lawmakers shuffle into their assigned positions. They exhibit a buoyant mood, an optimism that contrasts oddly with the unfailingly pessimistic forensics that launch a session ("Where will the money come from?"). The buoyancy has a vaguely incongruous lilt, too, in the aura of paltriness that mars the physical surroundings. Inside state capitols generally lies an almost studied atmosphere of shabbiness; nooks and cubbyholes where custodians post the relics of state that more often emit the scent of disinfectant than the fragrance of history. The innocent takes the condition to be a result of legislative frugality.

As a session gets rolling legislators look as they might in their full-time roles as lawyers, insurance men, merchants, bankers. Perhaps a bit more spruced up. But it is only at the start, before most members have submitted to capital city barbers, that one can stand at the rear of the chamber and guess, from the neckline of the haircuts, which members come from the cities and which from the boondocks. At first, small-town lawmakers tend to have shinier necks. Their neckties also tend to be wider, albeit the Founding Fathers probably did not plan it that way. As between the house and senate, one finds, on the average, wider neckties in the upper chamber.

Senators tend to be older and more conservative in

their dress. They also tend to be fatter, gruffer, more sedate, more pompous, windier, craftier, more willful and self-satisfied, more arrogant and self-important. They tend to be stingier at times and more extravagant at others. It depends on whether they are bilking or milking, both of which they do with greater frequency and higher facility but with fewer qualms. Senators tend to hold their opinions more staunchly simply because they shut out ideas more effectively. They are more resourceful. They sag into their great chairs with proprietary ease, and when they lug themselves up to speak they issue dicta on constitutional law and introduce visiting high school classes with equal emphasis, equal dignity, equal forensic power and equal relevancy to the issues. Senators manifest greater pretensions of culture and gentility. In New Jersey only the senators on opening day wear morning clothes. In Illinois, only the senators have brass spittoons. No matter what they are like in real life, state senators tend to become all these things because, everywhere except in unicameral Nebraska, they are the Upper Chamber. They also wear squeakier shoes than House members. An innocent learns all this gradually.

Younger and more numerous, members of the Lower Chamber tend to be more unruly and impulsive. It was the presiding officer of the Arkansas *house* who stabbed a contentious member to death. It was from the Illinois *house* that Lincoln leaped. House members tend to be rambunctious. Their debates tend to be louder, their hours longer, their humor gamier, their secretaries prettier. Their mistakes tend to be bigger. When they get drunk in the chamber they tend to get drunker in the chamber than senators. When they applaud a speech they usually applaud more fervently than it merits; when they make one they generally speak more loudly than it merits. Whatever they are like in real life, state representatives tend to take on these attributes when they become members of the Lower Chamber. They tend to become younger: one southern legislature expelled a middle-aged freshman for propositioning a twelve-year-old page girl. On the other hand, a legislator who gets promoted from the House to the Senate may altogether lose his interest in adolescent girls. Such characteristics become evident only gradually.

On the surface the legislature appears equipped, physically at least, to perform the duties assigned to it by the theory, philosophy and doctrine that one encounters in conventional governmental lore. It seems to be composed and organized to function in accordance with certain widely held propositions, premises and suppositions.

By the light of various preconceptions, the innocent expects, for example, to discover that the legislature complies with the state and federal constitutions; to find that the committee system works as a distilling process to improve legislation; and to see the bicameral system exhibit its widely admired capacity to check the passage of bad laws and balance one house's folly with another's wisdom. The innocent has heard, among other things, that legislatures practice economy, and he watches for this in what is known as the budget-making process. His presuppositions include premises that anyone will recognize as part and parcel of our governmental and political lore. Items:

The legislature is a democratic institution.

The legislature carries out the will of the people.

Committees conduct public hearings on proposed measures so that the popular will may be determined.

Because of malapportionment rural lawmakers dominate the legislature.

A rural-urban conflict is built into the legislative process.

The legislature is inefficient because it is understaffed.

The customary end-of-the-session rush shows that the legislature is overworked.

Such lore is widely believed. As the patient innocent gradually perceives, however, such theories bear little resemblance to actuality. The resemblance, such as it is, is superficial.

The check-and-balance theory of bicameralism, for example, flickers away into phantom nothingness, as though in a tricky maze of mirrors. When one house kills an important measure of the other, most often the initiating house had no expectation whatever that it would be enacted. Further, it is a commonplace for sponsors of legislation in one house to obtain the death of it in the other. On matters of consequence the two houses may well appear to be "checking" each other; there may be much killing of particular legislation. Usually, however, they conspire on spending matters and collude on tax measures.

The committee system turns out to be another instance of institutional sleight-of-hand. Day after day committees meet, in nook-and-cranny offices, in big rooms and small, and the innocent is frequently persuaded that here is being done the real homework of the legislature, here is the distillation process. Eventually he learns that the fate of very nearly every piece of major legislation is determined *before* its committee assignment; the destiny of bills already fated for death is often indicated *by* a committee assignment.

But the hearings, the public hearings? He learns that the more controversial the measure and the more elaborate the hearing, the more certain it is that the fate of the measure was predetermined before the hearing began.

As he learns about the committee system the innocent can hardly avoid disenchantment with the legend of legislative economy. Stingy the legislature is; *economical* it is not. The word suggests a methodical, prudent balancing of resources and needs. And, to be sure, appropriations committees conduct elaborate hearings, ostensibly to discover the needs and wants of the state. Wherever it occurs this drama produces the illusion that a government of reason is at work. There is every appearance of reasonable, judicious, prudent weighing and balancing. But the drama is almost pure theater. The content of the hearings will be seen to have little relevancy to the spending bills. Demonstrably, such bills almost always reflect not studied economy but the more or less arbitrary wishes of the legislative leaders. Most often, appropriations bills are fabricated after the hearings are done—and usually after each house individually has acted on a bill prepared by its own appropriations committee. Usually an all-powerful conference committee works its own will on appropriations. A similar process is followed in taxation matters.

One by one, the innocent watches conventional suppositions fall away. The concept of the legislature as a democratic institution simply collapses. By every operating tradition it functions as an autocratic or oligarchic institution. Frequently one properly placed man can dictate the disposal of legislation (a fact that can be illustrated by countless examples, some of which will be related elsewhere). The internal power structure of itself undermines the proposition that the legislature carries out the will of the people— even though, obviously, a legislative autocracy *could*, if it chose, do so. It becomes further evident, however, that legislative matters are nearly invariably controlled by an extensive coalition of industrial, commercial and business groups. In the conventional lore, these groups are styled the "special interests." Still, the studious innocent eventually perceives them to be in truth more than that. Finally they emerge not merely as "interests" approaching the legislature as might anyone entitled to the right of petition. They emerge as the legislature's *true constituency*. The people stand as the *theoretical constituency*. The commercial community is the *true constituency*.

As one observes longer, lore that has accumulated around the reapportionment issue begins to lose validity. It remains true that arithmetic shows that rural legislators dominate the legislature—or did for generations. Such statistics are familiar to all. Yet the conventional notions of rural domination and rural-urban conflicts tend not to apply to the actual scheme of things. It becomes clear that the legislators who represent rural areas do not actually function as rural legislators. They do not often represent rural interests. In actual practice, like their urban colleagues, they serve the true constituency. One regularly finds these "rural" legislators supporting measures that advance the interests of the true constituency over the interests of the rural areas. Examples abound and will be detailed subsequently. One also discovers, on the other hand, that rural legislators do not habitually support legislation designed to help rural folk—until their fellow countrymen so organize themselves that they take on the characteristics of the other big corporations that make up the true constituency. Until the citrus growers of California and Florida had formed great corporate combines they received no more legislative benefits than the ordinary farmers receive today, which is little. "The work of state departments of agriculture," as Roy Victor Peel put it (in *State Government Today*), "is almost entirely of a nature supplementing the assistance of the federal government." In other words, little initiative in behalf of the farmer has flowed from the rural-dominated legislature.

A revealing corollary to the antirural bias of the supposedly rural representatives lies in the fact that urban legislators are regularly the ones who emerge as opponents of legislation for the benefit of urban districts. They promote urban programs only to the extent that it is tolerated by the same true constituency that shapes most important law. In most states it has been common to find the most vociferous opponents to urban renewal among city legislators. This is not really surprising, once one realizes that the city legislator opposing such a measure is speaking not for the people, the theoretical constituency, but for one component of the true constituency—the great realty interests.

Having discarded these and other elements of conventional lore, the no-longer-innocent observer should seek other explanations for the legislature's institutional facade. If the theory of bicameralism is largely bunk, then how account for it? If budget-making is actually a matter of hit-and-miss expediency, how account for the elaborate ritualistic proceedings that surround it? There are usually reasonable explanations for even unreasonable human behavior, and in these instances the observer should seek them out.

In this aim, legislators themselves are only indirectly helpful, usually unwittingly. With some few exceptions, legislators express unbudging belief in these various propositions that seem so empty of reality. Many a legislator is willing in private to describe how the system of having two houses actually works; yet, at the same time, most of these will insist that what exists falls within the meaning of the traditional concept of checks and balances. Only a numb legislator could be unaware of how appropriations bills are actually put together. Yet almost all will defend and justify the practice of conducting the long hearings which, they will admit, have little point in actuality.

To this point came an unusually revealing series of comments from New York legislators as the legislature in 1966 considered changing the form of appropriations hearings. "We should begin now," said Assemblyman Harvey M. Lifset of Albany, the Ways and Means Committee chairman, "to experiment with a format of public hearings that will *make public enlightenment a reality*." (Emphasis mine.) This prospect, said Senate Majority Leader Earl W. Brydges, would be "a most progressive *innovation*." (Mine.)

The observer will find most legislators only ambiguously helpful in providing some understanding of the apportionment struggle's deeper implications. Publicly they contend over the equity of "X" area having "Y" percentage of the total representation. Privately some legislators will acknowledge that actually representation relates neither to population nor geographic area but to the various segments of the commercial community that form the true constituency. Nevertheless, these legislators will go on and on discussing apportionment in terms of statistics and conventional theories.

After long scrutiny and reflection the observer begins to perceive that these arguments and analyses made by the legislators themselves manifest a persistent quality that is not unlike the argumentation found in theology. They tend instinctively to translate everything that relates to the legislature into theories and doctrines and abstract notions that have the elusive qualities of theology or metaphysics, the same remoteness from the events that are actually occurring on the face of the earth. Theologians have filled libraries with elaborate philosophical writings to explain why the God who created many cruel things remains a good lovable God. Legislators (among others) tend to fabricate elaborate doctrines and theories to take account of the actual activities of the legislature and still justify it as a democratic institution.

Theories and doctrines thus produced naturally fail to explain the behavior of the legislature. On the contrary, they tend to conceal the reality of what goes on. Further reflection may suggest to the observer that the creation of these doctrines and theories is an organic legislative function. Every human institution produces doctrine as needed to protect, justify and defend itself, as well as to dissemble certain of its behavior. It is improbable that the legislature could persist without producing such doctrine any more than could wrongdoing monarchies persist without inventing the doctrine that the king can do no wrong. The rebellious barons at Runnymede could hardly have enforced their own terms on the crown without advancing the doctrine of a law higher than kings.

It is precisely here that the observer should begin to perceive the legislature in terms of its own actuality rather than in terms of the theories and doctrines that clothe it. He should perceive it as an institutional organism whose behavior is determined not merely by the circumstances and mores of the time but, as well, by attitudes and habits and dogma and customs whose roots sometimes trail deep in antiquity.

To understand the actual behavior of such an institution one must always look behind its doctrine.

An abstract discussion of bicameralism helps one understand the state legislature no more than a treatise on the Trinity helps one understand the actual behavior of the

Christian church. Knowledge of the Trinity helps one understand the *ceremonials* of the church but not its actual role in society. Similarly, much conventional lore about the state legislature is useful primarily in understanding not the institutional reality but its external forms.

5

"UNFORTUNATELY, THE SUB-
TLETIES OF THE LEGISLA-
TIVE PROCESS ARE ONLY
BEGINNING TO BE CATA-
LOGUED BY THE BEHAV-
IORAL SCIENTISTS. . . ."
—Albert J. Abrams,
secretary of the
New York State Senate

★★★★★★★★★★★★★★★★★★★★★
★★★★★★★★★★★★★★★★★★★★★

In any effort to plumb the
deeper character of the state legislature one is all but
obliged to dismantle its facade element by element. The job
ultimately needs some deduction and diagnostic guesswork,
too. Customary methods of observation fail to reveal funda-
mentals. One can much more conveniently document visible
legislative behavior than construct a reasonable hypothesis
about the organic nature that accounts for it. Still, curiosity
is not generally satisfied by the existing writing and thinking on the subject of the states. It may be helpful to sketch
some of the shortcomings of the customary ways of looking
at the states as political entities.

This does not entail any sweeping disparagement of the
existing literature. It provides a great body of elementary
information. From it one can handily learn much of legislative procedures, the step-by-step path that a bill follows and
how committees fit into the legislative table of organization.
One can learn of parliamentary rules and obtain a vast store
of fascinating statistical data and technical lore—how various state legislatures convene at different times and for
differing terms, how many bills are introduced and how
many enacted, what time the Senate meets and under what
circumstances the House majority caucuses, how the gover-

nor communicates with the lawmakers. One can discover which states require lobbyists to register, which hold budget sessions apart from general sessions, which allow advance filing of bills, which provide office space for members, which pay legislators poorly (New Hampshire pays $200 for two years) and which well (New York at $25,000 per biennium). On the shelves of any worthwhile library there lies an abundance of theory, a surfeit of doctrine. There have also been a number of incisive studies of state political systems, including the role of the legislature therein. Legislative personnel have been analyzed in terms of occupation, education, ideology and income. State political personalities have been sketched and exposed and dissected in periodicals and volumes. It is possible, and revealing, to learn of the politicians who were able to master their states (Huey Long, Harry Byrd, Arthur Samish, Thomas Dewey, George Wallace), as well as of the masterful politicians who were not: Soapy Williams, LeRoy Collins, William Scranton. A wealth of lore is available. It is all instructive. It is all to be considered in these comments. Still, it seems to fall short. With it all the observer still confronts a conundrum: almost every legislative ailment is curable by the legislature, but little or nothing is done. Why not? What's the matter with them? One can harvest an abundance of particulars about the states, the legislatures, without really understanding the institution. We know nearly everything about them except, finally, what makes them tick.

Journalists and political scientists, for example, have repeatedly tried to understand state legislatures by carefully analyzing the trades and professions of the members. In this the operating premise seems to be that if one thoroughly understands the individuals who make up an institution one will therefore understand the institution. Hence it is figured that if one discovers that a legislature contains so many lawyers, so many businessmen, so many farmers, so many labor leaders and so forth, all this will illuminate the institution in which they sit.

One typical personnel analysis of the California legislature produced the following occupational profiles of the 1965 membership:

In the senate of forty members there were two full-time legislators, fifteen attorneys, one savings-and-loan executive, one title-business executive, one insurance man, one newspaper publisher, one general contractor, four businessmen, one citrus grower, one retired businessman, one exporter, one teacher, one college instructor, one rancher-businessman, one veterinarian, one milk distributor, one retired rancher, one physician-surgeon, one rancher, one hotel owner and two vacancies caused by the appointment of a lawyer-member to the bench and the death of a member who was a general contractor.

In the assembly of eighty members there were four full-time legislators, one industrial-relations consultant, one transportation supervisor, two investment men, one wholesale-hardware executive, thirty-one attorneys, two clergymen, six teachers, two farmers, one farmer-realtor, two realtors, seven businessmen, three college instructors, two engineers, five ranchers, one movie-production man, one lumber-business manager, one land developer, three insurance agents, one optometrist, one pharmacist, one radio announcer and one economist.

A similar occupational hodgepodge turns up in nearly every state. What is one to make of it?

This kind of analysis can be interesting but is useful only within narrow limits. A knowledge of the professional backgrounds of legislators is often valuable in analyzing particular committees, for example in scouting out the agents through which bankers control banking committees, as they usually do, and the insurance industry the committees that reign in that field.

In general, however, membership studies tend to reveal not much beyond the fact that a fairly typical legislature could be assembled by scooping up and mixing together a Rotary club, a couple of Kiwanis clubs, a Junior Chamber of Commerce, a small bar association, a Ruritan club and for good measure a sprinkling of educators and perhaps a delegate or two from the garden club, the AMA or the League of Women Voters. In New England, of course, one would be obliged to stir in a few professional village characters, and in parts of the South one should spice the recipe by mulling in a small chapter of the Ku Klux Klan.

The inadequacy of studying the state legislature by studying its members—of seeking truths about the institution through individual biography—is fundamental. It seems almost axiomatic that a mature and functioning organization can be understood better, more usefully, in terms of its own characteristics than of the individual characteristics of its members. A corollary to this is that the behavior of an individual within an organization also can be usefully understood in terms of the organization's characteristics. To illustrate, nobody is likely to comprehend the nature of the Catholic church by examining the individual characteristics of its priests; but one can understand much of the behavior of the priests by understanding the Catholic church. The usefulness of this way of looking at things will become clear to anyone who reflects how, in practice, the method is all but unconsciously used in regarding and understanding other organizations.

Consider a recent (1964) visit to New York of an organization containing several hundred thousand lawyers, doctors, insurance men, realtors, mechanics, show people, engineers, restaurateurs, politicians, publishers, policemen and clerks—among other persuasions and occupations. For several days in New York the members of this organization exhibited uncommon behavior. The members rode about the streets upon oddly constructed vehicles (midget-sized motorcars and unicycles among them); they entangled crowds of strangers in vast skeins of invisible thread; they jammed noisily into elevators and perpetrated a variety of practical jokes using buzzers, whistles and sirens; they blocked each other (along with strangers) into revolving doors; a group of them reportedly squirted each other with a fire extinguisher in one hotel suite.

None of this was a matter for alarm. The organization

was the Ancient Arabic Order of the Nobles of the Mystic
Shrine of North America—the Shriners. They wore floppy
green and red trousers, gaudy embroidered jackets. Each
member wore a maroon felt fez.

"Why a fez?" *Time* magazine wondered. "The most
dedicated Shriner is hard put to say. The reason is that the
history of the Shrine was invented after its founding, and
has been elaborated ever since."

Institutional doctrine is commonly invented after the
circumstances it describes. So it is with the Shriners. But the
point here is that there is no way on earth to understand the
Shriners simply by understanding the individual members.
One may select a supremely normal and average real-estate
man and safely wager that he will exhibit extraordinary and
bizarre behavior when he joins the Shriners. Though he
might be studiously sedate while merchandising houses to
customers, the moment the realtor puts on the fez and scar-
let blouse of his lodge he is likely to engage in antics that
would absolutely bewilder an observer ignorant of the nature of the organization. His behavior would be quite inexplicable except to an observer who understood the Shriners
—the organization, its traditions, its purposes. No amount
of knowledge about this realtor could explain the Shriners,
however.

Every person has seen acquaintances undergo transfor-
mations of varying degrees upon entering some organization. A bakery operator exhibits different characteristics
when he puts on his American Legion cap. In Scout uniform
a young boy takes on perceptible new characteristics that he
draws from the nature of the organization. Who, however,
would attempt to fathom the true nature of the American
Legion by examining the peculiarities of the bakery operator? Or try to plumb the character of the Boy Scouts by
tabulating the idiosyncrasies of the young boy? The institution itself must be comprehended.

Just so, one should seek to comprehend the state legislature. As an institution of long life it has characteristics
more controlling than the characteristics of the individual
members. One might say of the legislature what Key, in

American State Politics, said of systems of political leadership: that they have developed "gradually, by the cumulation of habits, by . . . trial and error, and from the determining context of the society. . . . They are maintained by the logic of their own being and are amenable to change . . . by the same more or less blind process through which they came into being." (Key only summarized this deterministic theory and added it "merits respect, if not complete concurrence.")

Once in the legislature a lawyer or optometrist or bus driver consciously or otherwise tends to behave according to some compelling institutional "logic," the sometimes written but often unwritten rules of the institution—including its barely articulated traditions, customs, mores and rituals. Within the institution the individual member is governed more than he governs. The exceptions, whether maverick or gadfly, are as anomalous as a pouting Shriner at a lodge party. In most instances the individual lawmaker's *legislative* behavior should be construed not so much as a clue to his own private character as a clue to some element in the legislature's inner character or nature—its institutional psyche.

Thus it is important to take thoughtful note of all manner of legislative behavior that to a casual observer might appear to be trivial and insignificant. Just as a psychiatrist had better note carefully if his patient bites his fingernails or pops his knuckles, the student of the legislature had better take note when the Senate of North Carolina even entertains a proposal to designate the bedbug as the state insect. It may well suggest something special about the legislature as an institution.

When that Florida lawyer-legislator solemnly declared, "Freedom of speech is a privilege, not a right," it was neither a joke nor a slip, for this was the point of his speech. But not a soul in the House bothered to rise and correct him. Instead, they shouted approval of the censorship bill he was sponsoring. This suggested a good deal about the legislature.

There come times when a single legislative twitch or

spasm will illuminate institutional vistas that lie beyond the reach of routine research.

It would be difficult, for instance, to invent a lampoon contrasting the theory and practice of bicameralism more effective than the Associated Press's brief deadpan report on the Pennsylvania legislature at the end of 1965 and the beginning of 1966. The Senate adjourned its 1965 session and at once, at the constitutionally fixed hour, opened the 1966 session—which meant the automatic death of all pending 1965 bills. Nonetheless, the house continued its 1965 session and passed thirty-nine pieces of legislation that could not conceivably become law.

As another example, no bleeding heart could satirize legislative sensibilities more effectively than by relating episodes from, as they say, true life. In Austin, Texas legislators who were about to appropriate several hundred thousand dollars to the state's animal wildlife board also heard officials testify that the state did not employ a single juvenile parole officer; thus children, on being released, were often returned to detention for want of supervision and guidance. It was at this point that a senator advanced a suggestion: why not put the delinquents under the animal wildlife board? His colleagues roared with laughter. Comparable hilarity bubbled up in a Florida hearing on prison conditions. The knee-slapper: one legislator suggested that, as an answer to the need for more cell space, psychopathic killers be placed in cells together. Could a couple of sick jokes reveal a fundamental legislative orientation? For a more direct measure of state legislative humanity one need look no further than state penal systems. Former federal prison chief James Bennett has described them in a word: feudal.

The conventional lore has persuaded Americans that something, obviously, is wrong with the American state legislature. Yet the malaise, whatever, is often diagnosed as a passing condition, one that may be cured by giving the legislators more pay or longer terms or more flexible constitutions or longer sessions or bigger staffs or more appreciative electorates.

There is a further persistent tendency to regard the condition of the state as though it only recently developed. A past of great vitality is commonly evoked by political rhetoric as a backdrop on which to project despair at the "decline" of the states, to help establish the premise that the states suddenly are in "crisis."

To a considerable extent such portrayals rest upon wistful conceptions of the past. It is a matter the observer should explore. I shall later. It can be done only by peeling away layers of doctrine.

6

★★★★★★★★★★★★★★★★★★★★★
★★★★★★★★★★★★★★★★★★★★★

"THE MOST LIMITED INVESTI-
GATION RAISES A SERIOUS
DOUBT WHETHER THERE
EVER WERE ANY GOOD OLD
DAYS IN STATE POLITICS."
—Key

★★★★★★★★★★★★★★★★★★★★★
★★★★★★★★★★★★★★★★★★★★★

Barry Goldwater sang the states' righters' old sweet song pure and simple, and it will be useful to quote a few paragraphs directly from his creed:

My view that the states must reclaim the rights granted to them in the Constitution has been fortified as I have flown across the United States many times in the past years.

My answer to those who say that the concentration of population calls for doing away with the concepts of the Tenth Amendment is to point to the vast expanses of New York state that are not inhabited, to the mile after mile in the Middle West and the South that, for all intents and purposes, represent vacant farm land. We have room to grow and room to expand in these United States if we have the courage of our forefathers to battle the elements, the initiative to pursue and express our individuality.

There is nothing that could advance the cause of individual freedom more than for the people to take back to themselves locally the responsibility for governing themselves, to disengage themselves as much as practically possible from the tentacles of an overpowering government in Washington.

The disease of government interference, which has reduced our states to vassals of Washington, has eaten its way into our free enterprise economy. . . .

In seeking a clearer look at the state the observer encounters no greater obstacle than the argument or discussion that is cast in doctrinal or ideological or theoretical terms; it is an obstacle typified by the Goldwater creed which is quoted for that purpose. One encounters no obstacle more frequently. As I comment on it I shall often simply use the word doctrine as a term that includes both theory and ideology.

Both history and contemporary public dialogues tend to carry a heavy burden of doctrine. Like smoke over the battlefield, great clouds of doctrine darken the whole arena of American politics and government. It must be dealt with.

The trouble with the doctrinaire element is that it tends to confuse, intrigue, bedazzle, frighten, deceive and inspire one—all without revealing very much about the actual nature of either politics or government. Moreover, such are our habits of political thought that even as we struggle to comprehend the nature of government we tend to lapse into the very doctrinal vocabulary that tends to conceal it.

This is doubtless a natural human tendency. Yet, for the observer who wishes to see simply how things work, how they actually are, it is useful to be aware of the tendency and curb it where possible. As well, he should be mindful that a huge portion of political literature and informal commentary to which he is exposed is cast in deceptive doctrinal terms. These have been fashioned for many reasons—to confuse, frighten, bedazzle, persuade or inspire —but seldom to inform.

I emphasize and reiterate this because it is so easy to forget. It is commonly forgotten even by, or perhaps particularly by, reporters who are supposed to scrutinize politics professionally. Because doctrinal disputes flick at one's deepest feelings and attitudes, it requires an act of will in the heat of a political campaign to draw back and remind oneself that the candidates are not talking about actuality. Invariably, they are talking about certain notions that they have experienced or wish others to experience.

An overwhelmingly preponderant portion of political oratory is pure doctrine. It does not describe things that have actually happened, or things that will happen. It does not describe situations that exist or will exist. It does not, in a word, inform. That is not its purpose. It excites and stirs enthusiasm, which is its purpose.

When a candidate promises that he will support the "free enterprise" system, for instance, he is not describing the actual economic organization of America. He is simply employing a revered doctrine to arouse support. An observer interested in learning about the economic organization could not afford to be deterred by the slogan, the doctrine. He should examine the actual operations and attitudes found within, say, the petroleum industry (wherein production has been regulated for three decades), the sugar industry (operating under legally prescribed quotas), the banking industry (controlled by Federal Reserve legislation) or, among others, the private utility companies which of course are licensed monopolies chartered by, and guaranteed a profit by, the governments. These are but a few of the elements in the economic organization to which a candidate refers when he mentions the "free enterprise" system.

Doctrine is not easy to cope with. It wafts about like fog. Much of our political education comes to us in the form of doctrine. In this country we are not accustomed to calling our education an indoctrination but that is what it sometimes amounts to, particularly in the lower schools. At kindergarten level pupils are taught that America is a democracy and democracy is always good, so salute the flag. This is doctrine. It is useful in helping the youngster establish an identity and starts building his morale as a citizen. It does not, however, reveal much about either democracy or America. In junior high civics a youngster will learn that his state has a legislature that is divided (except in Nebraska) into two houses and enacts laws for the benefit of the biggest part of the people, which is called majority rule. This is doctrine. It reveals little and includes a measure of deceit calculated to inspire the youngster to be a better citizen. The high school or college student becomes acquainted with the standard textbook presentation that usually recaps how the nation was founded, how the colonies grew into states and how they function under some arrangement called the system of federalism. More doctrine. It inculcates an impulse to marvel at the intricately balanced American "system" of federalism while postponing the day when the student will shake off his indoctrination long enough to perceive how the American scheme of government actually works.

At almost every turn doctrine blocks the way. It excites the observer with fanciful metaphor, beguiles him with webs of metaphysics, persuades him with shrewd semantics. Goldwater's creed is quoted at the outset of this segment because it illustrates a variety of the snares that lie in wait for the observer who is simply trying to take a cold look at the American state.

At its very semantic inception, of course, the states' rights doctrine was calculated to confuse. Nothing else could have resulted from the fact that its adherents misappropriated the word "rights," a word with perhaps more emotional content than any other in this country's political vocabulary. The fundamental justification of the American revolution is that individuals—not governments—are endowed with rights (doctrine that justified but hardly described our behavior toward the British). By oratorically endowing states with *rights* various American politicians automatically obtained considerable free emotional pulling power as they pressed their designs upon society. Had an eighteenth-century flack personally dreamed up this idea ("Hey, Mannie, why don't we get the antifeds to talk about states' *rights*, not this states' *powers* stuff? *Rights* is hot, *powers* don't sell!"), the early antifederalists probably would have paid him a fortune.

The modern antifederalist, of course, just as his ancestors did, is actually referring to state powers when he speaks of state rights. This is an important quibble. Under the Constitution, for instance, the southern Negro has long possessed the *right* to vote; he has heretofore often lacked the *power*.

In the wooly dialogue of political debate it is often forgotten that the Tenth Amendment—that states' righters hold to be so vital but whose sponsors declared was only a statement of the obvious—does not pertain to rights at all. It is brief. It says: "The *powers* not delegated to the United States by the Constitution nor prohibited by it to the States, are reserved to the States respectively, or to the people." On the other hand the Ninth Amendment pertains to residual *rights* ("The enumeration in the Constitution, of certain rights, shall not be construed to deny or disparage others retained by the people") and does not refer to the states at all.

Barry Goldwater's creed was anything but original. In our era it struck some as fresh only because it was so startlingly rudimentary. Doctrine like Goldwater's has proliferated in American political commentary since the beginning of the nation, and one gains the impression that it has increased in the last three decades. Beyond doubt it has fuzzed up the perceptions of many an observer.

To presume that a state possesses *rights* is to look upon it with undeserved reverence, to personify it, to feel awe about it, as though it were a pulsing living thing. The conception helps induce deep and sympathetic emotions about an abstraction and to that extent deters thought about the thing itself. The state is not so complicated: a piece of land bounded by happenstantial lines and inhabited by people who by and large acquiesce in some community governance by elected delegates who are supposed to follow rules set down in a written code called the state constitution. To experience awe at this is probably harmless; but it also is to be distracted from watching it work. When President Eisenhower took office he too was all misty-eyed about states' rights. But by 1957 the mists had parted enough for him to discover how the states work: "Opposed though I am to needless federal expansion," he said, "since 1953 I have found it necessary to urge federal action in some areas traditionally reserved to the states. In each instance state inaction, or inadequate action . . . has forced emergency federal action."

Opposed though *he* was to federal action, Barry Goldwater did not see it quite the same way as Ike. In his creed government action became "the disease of government interference" and the federal establishment in Washington an "overpowering" creature that has "tentacles" reaching out; it has "reduced our states to vassals."

Very interesting. It tells something of Goldwater's notions but nothing whatever about either Washington or Phoenix.

7

"CAN WE FORGET FOR WHOM WE ARE FORMING A GOVERNMENT? IS IT FOR MEN, OR FOR THE IMAGINARY BEINGS CALLED STATES? WILL OUR HONEST CONSTITUENTS BE SATISFIED WITH METAPHYSICAL DISTINCTIONS?"

—James Wilson

"THE MERITS AND DEFECTS OF THE PROPOSED CONSTITUTION HAVE BEEN LARGELY AND ABLY DISCUSSED. FOR MYSELF, I WAS READY TO HAVE EMBRACED ANY TOLERABLE COMPROMISE THAT WAS COMPETENT TO SAVE US FROM IMPENDING RUIN. . . ."

—George Washington

★★★★★★★★★★★★★★★★★★★★
★★★★★★★★★★★★★★★★★★★★

The states' rights controversy has rumbled right along. It is going on two centuries now. Its duration alone might suggest that here is a matter of great importance. Certainly if the controversy has revealed anything of importance about the states the observer should seek it out.

It has proved at least the rare adaptability of doctrinaire argument. This is shown by one intriguing difference between the antifederalist of today and his eighteenth-century soulmate.

Today's antifederalist insists that under the U.S. Constitution the states retain full sovereignty, an elusive property which, of course, they contend is being encroached upon by a federal establishment that was never intended to be a consolidated government.

The eighteenth-century antifederalist, however, insisted that the U.S. Constitution effectively demolished the states by creating a central government that was national rather than federal in character.

"This government," said Patrick Henry, a bitter foe of the new Constitution, "is not a Virginian, but an American government. Is it not, therefore, a consolidated government?" He was so persuaded.

After Pennsylvania's convention ratified the Constitution the antifederalist faction issued a dissent asserting among other things "that the new government will not be a confederacy of States, as it ought, but one consolidated government, founded upon the destruction of the several governments of the States. . . ."

"The very idea," said Virginia's George Mason, "of converting what was formerly a confederation, to a consolidated government, is totally subversive of every principle which has hitherto governed us. This power is calculated to annihilate totally the state governments."

Great volumes of such testimony have been assembled. A fair summary of the antifederalist position was that the Constitution would effectively destroy the states. The observer should not worry about the merit of this old argument. The object here is to perceive, at length, the various ways in which doctrine is spread over actuality.

An important issue in the pre-Constitution debates was the implication of the phrase, "We the People," as it appears in the Constitution. Antifederalists of that day felt that this language wiped out the states. "Had it said 'We the States,'" declared a member of the North Carolina ratifying convention, "there would have been a federal intention in it. But, sir, it is clear that a consolidation is intended." A Massachusetts antifederalist was equally emphatic about the import of employing "We the People" instead of "We the States":

If it "does not go on to an annihilation of the state governments, and to a perfect consolidation of the whole union," he said, "I do not know what does."

This kind of point seemed to be clearly understood. On the other side there were citizens like the North Carolina delegate who said: "One of the . . . objections to the Constitution . . . is that it is not the act of the states but of the people, but that it ought to be the act of the states. . . . I hope, sir, that all power is in the people, and not in the state governments."

Then, too, there were practical politicians like Elbridge Gerry, who scoffed at the whole abstract debate. "We never were independent states," he said, "we're not such now, & never could be even on principles of the Confederation." The states' righters, he added, were "intoxicated with the idea of their *sovereignty*." (His emphasis.)

Today's antifederalists are still intoxicated with the idea of state sovereignty. But in spinning the doctrine to defend it, they take quite the opposite position from yesterday's antifederalist. They insist that the Constitution did *not* establish a consolidated government. Bolstering this position they take a different reading on what "We the People" means.

"Of course," writes one prominent states' righter, Richmond editor James J. Kilpatrick, " 'We the People' meant . . . 'We the people *of the states*.' " (Now, why in hell couldn't the early antifederalists see *that*?) Anyway, Kilpatrick, who helped revive the doctrine of interposition in the mid-1950s, elaborates the point in his book called *The Sovereign States*. He writes:

"The self-evident fact . . . was that the *whole* people, the mass of people from Georgia to New Hampshire, obviously had nothing to do with the ratification of the Constitution. . . . Ratification was achieved by the people of the States, acting in their sovereign capacity not as 'Americans,' for there is no 'State of America,' but in their sovereign capacity as citizens of the States of Massachusetts, New York, Virginia, and Georgia."

Naturally, Kilpatrick concludes that the Constitution

did *not* establish a consolidated government. "The argument here," he writes, "is that the States, in forming a new perpetual union to replace their old perpetual union, remained in essence what they had been before: separate, free, and independent States. They *surrendered* nothing to the Federal government they created. *Some of their powers they delegated; all of their sovereignty they retained.* [Emphasis his.] It is keenly important that this distinction be understood. There is a difference between 'sovereignty' and 'sovereign power.'"

While the observer may fret over why Patrick Henry and others *thought* they were surrendering so much, he should not worry too much about the difference between "sovereignty" and "sovereign power." It is not keenly important to know the difference. Nor is it keenly important to know what Kilpatrick means when he writes that "sovereignty is the moving river" and "the wind that blows" and "the life spirit" and "the soul"—albeit a substance that "can be divided, when two States are created of one." This should be enjoyed as tolerable poesy and middling metaphysics. It relies heavily on Calhoun, who differs to the extent of maintaining "that sovereignty is in its nature indivisible. . . . We might just as well speak of half a square, or half a triangle, as of half a sovereignty."

We might just as well, at that.

What is important to glimpse is the actuality behind the doctrine. When Kilpatrick was spinning his fine abstractions, he was actually defending the Virginia government's attempts to keep Negroes out of white schools. The Negroes were not abstract, however, and neither were the schools into which the federal courts ultimately got them. Under the circumstances, the shading between "sovereignty" and "sovereign power" made no difference at all.

Neither the courts nor the Negroes were satisfied with metaphysical distinctions. The observer should not be either.

The temptation to delineate the place of the state in the federal system is almost irresistible. Few commentators resist it. There is a vast literature in which philosophers and politicians set out to accomplish the chore.

The metes and bounds of the states have been set down in terms of functions, powers, prerogatives, purposes and rights. They have been adumbrated in the legalistic jargon of the courts and celebrated in the wispy metaphysics of political partisans. All these efforts have one thing in common: they are debatable.

When Hamilton and Madison were writing the Federalist Papers to help sell the new constitution they had a splendid go at defining everything—before it was possible for anybody on earth to know what might develop.

"The federal Constitution forms a happy combination," said Madison, ". . . the great and aggregate interests being referred to the national, and the local and particular to the state legislatures."

There was little to quarrel over in this—except which interests were local, which particular, which great, which aggregate. Madison, for whom one of New York's great avenues is named, was a better salesman of the Constitution than a prophet of its effects. It is plain from the archives of the law and the history of the Civil War that the combination has not invariably been a happy one. Perhaps history alone justifies the yearning for definitude, a yearning that brought into being the layer-cake theory of American federalism—or, as former Minnesota Governor Orville L. Freeman called it, "the layer-cake absolute that calls for neat division between federal and state governments. This myth," Freeman went on in a 1963 speech, "ought to have been demolished by decades of repudiation in practice, but there is still a widespread wistful notion that all this is temporary and that one of these days, when we just put our minds to it, we will sort out the functions of government and put the cake back into the proper layers."

This wistful notion could be heard when Pennsylvania's Governor William Scranton addressed the New York Chamber of Commerce in 1966. "We need," he said, "a reappraisal of the respective responsibilities of the different levels of government—particularly a thorough appreciation of the vital role of state government." President Eisenhower thought so, too, and in 1957 got the Governors Conference to set in motion a joint Federal-State Action Commission to study this matter. After a year of study the committee begat a report and little else. "It turned out to be an exercise in futility," said one member, LeRoy Collins. Its most earth-shattering proposal was that the federal government might consider abandoning aid for the building of sewage treatment plants.

Scranton's proposal, in the light of that very recent experience, only proves the durability of the wistful desire for order, for some evidence that things in the American scheme are logically and rationally arranged. He may well feel that a "reappraisal" will establish that this is the realm of the state, that the realm of the federal government, and there the realm of the locality.

His quest is altogether human. A comparable yearning for a sense of perfection has been the single most persistent characteristic of mankind's religious life. To satisfy it theologians and preachers have fashioned appealing stories about places where perfection and order prevail, places like heaven and Eden. Only in this way can such yearnings be fulfilled.

In mankind's political and social life, similarly, this yearning for order has produced a variety of familiar and frankly imaginary utopias. It has also produced doctrine that is no less utopian for purporting to describe actual conditions. Emotions of almost a religious quality attach to many of the central doctrines that occur in American political life. The central doctrines are the verities; no intelligent politician ever criticizes them even if he disbelieves them. Political craft consists of doing what must be done in the name of the verities; political folly consists of admitting that what was thought to be absolute and eternal has been long since abandoned. It was hardly surprising that as the federal government took on major new tasks in the New Deal FDR insisted this was "cooperative federalism." A comparable political wisdom has prompted President Johnson to couple his mammoth new Great Society ventures with a simultaneous insistence that he stands for "creative federalism." Creative federalism—"fluid in design and flexible in application," it was said to be. No doubt. What this is, of course, is creative flapdoodle. The notion of federalism is one of the American verities, and Mr. Johnson is not about to give way to iconoclasm this late in life.

The concept of the American political scheme as an *ordered* federalism is, of course, a utopian notion, which is precisely why scholars and politicians are still arguing about it. If an ordered federalism had ever come into actual being we would not still be debating whether it exists or, if it does, what its nature is.

One effect of the ceaseless debate has been to generalize the way we habitually think of the states; the tendency, when one attempts to settle the place of states in a utopian federalism, is to abstract and idealize them. Religious doctrine similarly conditions us to think abstractly and ideally about certain institutions of the church—marriage, for example. The idealization helps jewelers sell a lot of merchandise through ads depicting the glowing bride and groom, but it does not reveal much about the nature of marriage.

From time to time someone comes along and announces that federalism is done with, faded away, dead. Even they, of course, are obliged to assume that it once existed, functioned and even flourished. Whatever the merit of them, such pronouncements have generated fantastic quantities of controversy among politicians and students of government.

It was in 1939 that Harold Laski declared on a visit to the U.S. that "the epic of federalism is over. . . ." Federalism, he added, "is insufficiently positive in character; it does not provide for sufficient rapidity of action; it inhibits the emergence of necessary standards of uniformity; it relies upon compact and compromise . . . ; its psychological results, especially in an age of crisis, are depressing to a democracy that needs the drama of positive achievement to retain its faith." At the time, naturally, there was a great rumble of rebuttal. It was not necessary to prove that federalism had ever actually functioned. That seemed to be established by Laski's assertion that it had stopped functioning.

What the observer may find interesting, however, is that the rebuttal has not stopped. ". . . The states are not on the governmental junk-heap," declared Oregon's Governor Mark O. Hatfield. In a speech to the National Municipal League, Hatfield was replying specifically to Laski's observations—twenty years after Laski made them.

As late as 1963 Nelson A. Rockefeller found it timely, in a series of lectures at Harvard, to reply specifically to Laski. Rockefeller insisted that federalism is, too, alive. He explained:

> The federal idea: what does this mean?

> Let me first make it clear that I do not speak of the federal idea as merely a *mechanical or technical or abstract formula for government operations.* [My emphasis.]

> I refer to the federal idea broadly as a concept of government by which a sovereign people, for their great progress and protection, yield a portion of their sovereignty to a political system that has more than one center of sovereign power, energy, and creativity. No one of these centers or levels has the power to destroy another. Under the Constitution, for example, there are two principal centers of government power—state and federal. As a practical matter, local government, by delegation of state authority under the principle of "home rule," is a third such key center of power. The federal idea, then, is above all an idea of a shared sovereignty at all times responsive to the needs and will of the people in whom sovereignty ultimately resides.

Just so did Rockefeller digest a *mechanical* and *technical* and *abstract* formula for government. No tolerant person could be offended by this. It tends, in truth, to alleviate one's yearning for order.

It is pleasant to believe that somewhere out there lies an immense pool of sovereignty from which, as though it were a great pool of oil, a certain amount is piped into the national capital and a certain portion into the state capitals. The trouble is, as Rockefeller ought to know, that when one is pumping something, even something as palpable as oil, there is no certainty that it will reach its destination with either its proprietary or economic properties unaltered, if it reaches its destination at all.

In the 1870s a group of producers obtaining oil at the big Bradford Field in Pennsylvania tried to avoid becoming prisoners of the Standard Oil Trust, which controlled railroad rates, by building a pipeline over the Alleghenies and to the sea. When this facility, the Tidewater Pipe Line, was completed, and when its proprietors refused John D. Rockefeller's offer to buy all their oil, Standard began building its own pipeline that ran into an obstacle at the town of Bayonne; oddly enough, a railroad that went through there opposed the crossing of the pipeline. Standard responded to this by persuading the mayor and town council of Bayonne to be extraordinarily cooperative. As Matthew Josephson related in *The Robber Barons*, the town council speedily and secretly granted Standard's agents a franchise while Standard's construction crews stood at the ready. Then on the night of September 22, 1879, before the railroad could obtain a blocking order, the crews laid the new pipeline through Bayonne and onward to the sea. Soon the Tidewater company experienced so much financial difficulty that it sold its pipeline to Standard.

Sovereignty is more slippery than oil.

8

"THE LIFE OF LAW HAS NOT
BEEN LOGIC; IT HAS BEEN
EXPERIENCE."
—Oliver Wendell Holmes

★★★★★★★★★★★★★★★★★★★
★★★★★★★★★★★★★★★★★★★

Whatever sovereignty is, it is not permanent. That can be put down as an axiom. One supposes that the Crown has already taken note of this truth. Some surviving antifederalists seem not so easily persuaded. Some of this era's most damaging domestic stress has resulted from political actions that *seemed* to be predicated on the assumption that the American states possess what is called sovereignty.

For centuries politicians have been inflamed by the word, theoreticians have been enamoured of it. Yet, amidst all this flaming passion over sovereignty the only ones regularly swived have been the people. "Popular sovereignty," as Arthur Bromage wrote of an earlier era, "was more nearly property sovereignty." The observer is obliged to deal with the subject of sovereignty.

Actually, the notion of sovereignty is not as remote and abstruse as it is sometimes made to seem. It appears most abstruse, usually, when someone is trying to prove that it exists where it does not. This accounts for the complexity of the arguments through which antifederalists attempt to prove that the states are sovereign.

In 1576 Bodin defined sovereignty as the "supreme power over citizens," and the common meaning has not changed despite the intricate shadings that generations of partisans have attempted to impose upon the word. By the only useful meaning of the word a totally innocent observer might wonder how anyone, following the establishment of the national government, could have supposed that the American states possessed sovereignty. Yet a great chunk of the history of the country tells of events flowing from that supposition. It seemingly persists to this day, as the files on Orval Faubus, Ross Barnett and George Wallace prove.

Sovereignty, however, is as simple as Bodin made it sound. And it is either there or it is not. To establish sovereignty is simply to assert the right to run things—while demonstrating the will and intention and readiness and capacity to raise superior hell if need be to do so. At Runnymede the barons possessed the will and wherewithal to accomplish their purpose whatever the king said. This drift of things did not escape John. His majesty chose to retain the semblance of sovereignty rather than assert the real thing. When it comes to mean anything sovereignty is not abstract at all. In truth, it tends to become mischievous when it is abstracted.

With infinitely imaginative abstractions Calhoun helped convince the South that the states did possess sovereignty. This did not matter in the least so long as the states did not act on this belief. When they did, sovereignty proved to be something more than rhetoric. The southern states had everything they needed to prove themselves sovereign except one: the wherewithal. Without that they proved to have no sovereignty at all.

To assume today that the states possess sovereignty is silly. For state governments to act on the assumption can be profoundly mischievous. The last decade has provided several illustrations of this. Little Rock, Ole Miss, the University of Alabama are primary examples.

Reflecting on these examples, the observer may be struck by a thought that seems obvious: namely, that it has been so clear for so long that the states did not possess sovereignty that no rational politician could really have *believed* the contrary.

The thought justifies further analysis. After all, it *is* incredible; it is impossible to conclude that the governors of Arkansas, Mississippi and Alabama *believed* that these states were sovereign, that they would be supreme, that they would prevail in the segregation confrontations at Little Rock, Oxford and Tuscaloosa.

This is self-evident. It is equally obvious that a sovereignty that does not intend to establish supremacy no longer really stands as a sovereignty. Just as obviously, Faubus, Barnett and Wallace did not intend to establish supremacy over the federal government, even though their acts of defiance appeared to rest upon the invocation of state sovereignty.

A multitude of facts, of course, show that they did not believe as they appeared to believe. As soon as the federal establishment called his hand Faubus folded. Barnett hoped to retreat in a charade, which he discussed in detail with the U.S. attorney general, Robert Kennedy; they even debated whether federal marshals on their arrival at Ole Miss should draw their pistols or merely place their hands on them. Barnett's charade, unfortunately, disintegrated into the Ole Miss rioting. At Tuscaloosa, however, Wallace's came off as slickly as a television soap opera. It all went according to script: Wallace placed himself in the "school house door" to prevent the admission of a Negro. But he had no intention whatever of actually preventing the admission, no intention of prevailing. Despite his rhetoric, it was not an assertion of state sovereignty.

Then what was all this about?

Essentially, Faubus and Barnett and Wallace were only dramatizing or celebrating the contemporary orthodoxy of the community. To understand this is not to forget that the results of so doing were grave. Symbolic actions often are among the most dangerous. The U.S. presence in Berlin, as a large example, is symbolic; the country is dramatizing a policy; it is dangerous to do so. Symbolic acts often lead individuals into difficulty. In the mid-1960s numerous youths are burning their draft cards to dramatize their pacifism; some end up in trouble with the law. The violent events at Little Rock and Ole Miss do not alter the fact that these state governors, rather than actually asserting sovereignty, were but dramatizing community orthodoxy.

It is useful to view their actions in these terms. It should lead the observer to a clearer understanding of the nature of the states, of some of the ways in which they actually function in the American society.

I refer here not to constitutional functions or statutory functions—but to certain functions that have devolved upon the state as one of the institutions within the society. These are functions that the state apparatus performs not methodically and rationally but intuitively, unconsciously.

In the organic development of a society there is little deliberation about the distribution of functions among the various institutions that come into existence. Still, institutions seem to pick up some subliminal cue flashed by some unarticulated need. Museums become the custodians of obsolete but revered esthetic values, and from time to time they march them out and celebrate them—while show business and Madison Avenue establish the esthetic values actually in use. Nobody sat down and decided that these institutions should fulfill these functions. The church, assisted by happy-ever-after fiction and movies and sterling silver advertisements, nurtures society's fading (but still dear) notions about marriage—while an elaborate subinstitution within the law, symbolized by the divorce machinery in Reno, fulfills the services required by society's actual operating beliefs about marriage.

The observer should not spend time moralizing about these things. It will change nothing. Institutions take on these functions in response to real needs that are not going to vanish in the face of preaching. Though unarticulated, such societal needs will be fulfilled.

One such need is for the dramatization or celebration of orthodoxy when it is menaced or appears to be. In this country the state frequently fulfills this need. In the illustrations related above, the governor became the key agent in performing this function. More usually, it is the state legislature. Once the observer recognizes this, much legislative behavior that has seemed incomprehensible, futile or silly will suddenly become understandable.

One of the most illuminating books I ever read on the subject of government was one that Thurman W. Arnold published in 1935. It is called *The Symbols of Government* and it begins with these sentences:

"The principles of Washington's farewell address are still sources of wisdom when cures for social ills are sought. The methods of Washington's physician, however, are no longer studied. Political and legal science only look to the past."

Later Arnold adds: "It is only natural that our governmental scholars should go back to the learning of the past. The confusing events of their own day constantly contradict their most fundamental assumptions. The road to discovery is thus closed to all who refuse to accept the world as it is."

So it seems. But one trouble is that an intricate web of doctrine veils the world-as-it-is. It is as hard to see as to accept. Actuality is more palatable in the costumery of abstractions. Political commentary reeks of doctrine, and the doctrine is saturate with history. Doctrine is woven of the notions and ideas that are dear to the people. Fluid and disturbing contemporary events seem more tolerable when described in the language of dear old notions. A sense of permanence is thus lent to things. Doctrine has about it, as well, a quality of euphemism. Politicians, among others, often find it easier to defend a doctrinal principle—of which any variety of contradictory ones are available—than to defend some distasteful actuality.

In one era many Americans effectively advocated cheap child labor simply by objecting that it was unconstitutional to prohibit it; the legalistic debate saved them the embarrassment of insisting that kids be kept in the sweatshops. "At one time or another," wrote Professors Alfred Kelly and Winfred Harbison in *The American Constitution*, "every economic interest, every geographical section, and almost every state, expounded a theory of states' rights to justify its opposition to the prevailing policies of the federal government. Likewise, every interest, section, and state supported some federal measures of a strongly nationalistic character, and practically every state eventually went on record in condemnation of what it considered an excessive states' rights position of a sister state." In one symposium, Florida's LeRoy Collins provided a specific illustration of the use of doctrine as a smoke screen. "Minimum wages are a good example," he said. "Those economic interests which have opposed—in the name of states' rights—every single effort at the federal level to provide American citizens assurance of decent minimum wages have not encouraged the state governments to provide such. It is not really 'federal encroachment' they oppose: it is minimum wages." Thurmond Arnold wryly related how the debate over Prohibition tended to be transformed from an argument over whisky to a high-flying discussion of the principles of law enforcement. "For every 'dry' speech on the dangers of disobedience," he wrote, "there was a 'wet' oration on the dangers of invading the privacy of the home."

It is useful for the observer to note such instances in which doctrine is merely the distorted shadow of the substance of events. He should know then that doctrine will never carry him to an understanding of the states. Still, he will be obliged to penetrate a great deal of doctrine to reach some understanding. The effort should not be regarded as a debunking operation. One should emulate the attitude of the detached spectator who wishes to see the world as it is (actuality) as well as what it says it is (doctrine). One also must adjust to the paradox that even though what the world *says* is often intended to conceal what it *is,* what it *says* is also inevitably part and parcel of what it *is.*

Thus the object of study should be not to demolish doctrine but to perceive where it is used for dissembling, where it is a symptom of wistful hopes and, perhaps, where it actually reflects a controlling attitude that lies somewhere in the legislative character or psyche.

This deeper understanding, after all, is the goal of these ruminations. It does not require endless quibbling. It requires the examination of sufficient detail to remove the mystery from the conventional and historic vocabulary of American politics. One need not quarrel with the proposition that there exists somewhere out there in America a great pool of sovereignty, residing in some mystical way with the people. The premise is inextricably bound up in the assertion that a higher, unearthly power has endowed us with our rights.

Such is mankind's congenital attitude toward authority that men have always found it necessary to employ some such assertion when breaking free of unwanted temporal control. The Protestants freed themselves from the mother church by asserting that they were now getting the word directly from God. Similarly the barons had to invoke a law above King John. From time immemorial human beings have been invoking higher powers, always unseen and unprovable, to justify what they intend to do. On a trite level, one of the most universal set pieces in fiction or life is that in which two people who are either in love or impassioned decide to commit adultery after deciding, "It's bigger than both of us." This higher law makes it all right.

Man has a boundless, bottomless inventiveness that supplies the doctrines he needs to justify what he has done or intends to do. He is always quick to authenticate the ideas that he holds about himself. He wishes to appear reasonable. He has "a decent respect to the opinions of mankind."

It is futile to disparage mankind's slogans and stupid to ignore them. Still, it is perhaps useful to see them for what they are.

9

"THE VENERATION WE
RIGHTLY FEEL FOR THE CON-
STITUTION MAKES EXPLORA-
TION IN DEPTH OF OUR
POLITICAL SYSTEM SEEM
ALMOST SACRILEGIOUS."
—Hyman G. Rickover

★★★★★★★★★★★★★★★★★★★★
★★★★★★★★★★★★★★★★★★★★

At this point I suggest, as an
axiom the observer will find useful, the following:

*One intuitive institutional function of the state legis-
lature is to celebrate community orthodoxy (1) when it
appears to be menaced, (2) when it is actually menaced,
(3) when it is crumbling, (4) when it is actually obsolete
but still revered as a tenet of the community creed.*

It will become apparent to the observer that this axiom
accounts for an extensive variety of legislative behavior that
otherwise appears baffling, irrational, pointless, impractical
and sometimes downright lunatic. On reflection the observer will see that no other institution in American society
performs this function in quite the same way.

To be sure, the courts do function as a forum for the
celebration of community orthodoxy. "For most persons," as
Thurman Arnold put it, "the criminal trial overshadows all
other ceremonies as a dramatization of the values of our
spiritual government." There is a difference, however, in
this function of the courts. They dramatize the orthodoxy as
it exists at the moment, the presently prevailing values.
Usually, with some lag, the courts will also provide a dramatization of changing orthodoxy. When American business
was ruthlessly abiding by Herbert Spencer's survival-of-the-
fittest code of the jungle, it was Justice Holmes who reminded the country: "The Fourteenth Amendment does not

enact Mr. Herbert Spencer's Social Statics." More recent
and dramatic is the way the courts have functioned in the
recent years of changing values in race relations. Their performance contrasts sharply with that of the state legislature
in the South.

The state legislature does not tend to celebrate community orthodoxy by adjusting to it when it is changing. It
celebrates the passing orthodoxy, that which is obsolete but
still of emotional value to the community or to a substantial
part of it that cannot fully adapt to a new operating orthodoxy. From common observation, one might conclude that
the state legislature celebrates orthodoxy with the greatest
intensity when, from a practical viewpoint, it is most useless
to do so—that is, when the orthodoxy is ripely obsolescent.

In any event, this axiom may assist the observer in com-
prehending legislative behavior that many have despaired
of understanding. Here, to be elaborated on later, is a summary of certain legislative behavior to which this axiom may
be applied:

1. It accounts for the fact that the state legislature ad-
heres to economic doctrine long since discarded by American society. In a nation thriving on principles of borrowing
and spending, the state legislature is the only important institution in which the old cash-and-carry notions of thrift
and debtlessness (dear to every mortgaged American) are
still celebrated. Every legislature in every session can be
counted on to set the stage and celebrate this obsolescent
economic orthodoxy—while our friends at Chase Manhattan buy valuable television time to implore customers to
come in and borrow.

2. It accounts for the fact that the state legislature regularly surrenders to the impulse to play the part of the
censor, the defender of purity, old style. The legislature almost invariably celebrates the old standard when a new is
taking hold. New Jersey's legislature enacted the silly, un-
workable antismut bill quoted earlier at a time when few
intelligent Americans even blink at a novel like *Candy*. The
Florida legislature pressed an intensive investigation of sex-

ual behavior on college campuses in an era when every mass magazine is discovering at least once a year that the old sex code is dead.

3. It accounts for the fact that the state legislature regularly manifests a witch-hunt syndrome, becoming the inquisitor, the heresy hunter. For fifty years the state legislature's witch-hunt syndrome has made Washington's spate of McCarthyism seem in comparison like a mere fleeting aberration. Invariably, the witch-hunt syndrome appears when orthodoxy is changing. By hunting witches the legislature celebrates the old, still dear orthodoxy. During the Depression, when the whole fabric of the American creed was shredding, no less than forty-four states wasted vast energy debating loyalty oaths and sedition laws. California alone enacted a sedition law under which around five hundred persons were jailed—something McCarthy at his hottest never accomplished.

4. It accounts for the fact that the state legislature recurringly manifests a thought-control syndrome, which, of course, is closely kin to the witch-hunt syndrome. The thought-control syndrome, however, is characterized by legislative efforts to intrude into the internal affairs of institutions actually under public control. When this syndrome is activated the legislature acts as though it would curtail freedom at state universities and colleges; it begins to screen public school textbooks and library books for sedition and subversive influences. When any of this occurs, it will be observed that someone or some idea is challenging the community orthodoxy. In these thought-control quests the legislature does a great deal of harm, but it never accomplishes anything. That is not the underlying purpose. It is simply celebrating orthodoxy.

Legislative conduct of these varieties should be familiar to the observer no matter what his state. As these comments were being written in the winter of 1966 the Michigan Senate adopted a resolution asking "state-supported colleges and universities to deny their institutions as a forum for Communist speakers." The senate resolution was a prelude to the scheduled appearance at Wayne State University in Detroit and Michigan State University in East Lansing of Herbert Aptheker, director of the American Institute for Marxist Studies, New York. "This is only a resolution making a request of the colleges," said Senate Majority Leader Raymond Dzendzel after the Senate action, "but we hold the purse strings." The refrain is familiar to every state college in the land. So is this variety of action.

Many observers are puzzled by it simply because it so obviously never accomplishes anything. When a speech is actually cancelled the views of the speaker get more attention than they would have if normal standards of free speech had been allowed to prevail. When the speaker is nonetheless allowed to appear, as occurred in Michigan, his remarks also are given more widespread attention. It would libel the intelligence of the state legislature to assume that its members do not perceive this obvious fact. They do perceive it, of course, but it does not matter. What the legislature is doing in such an instance is celebrating orthodoxy.

In celebrating orthodoxy the legislature does not have to act decisively. The drama is the thing, the play, the public reaffirmation of fading community verities. In the case of the Michigan resolution just cited the vote was only 15 to 14, for example. Yet, the debate allowed everyone, whether for or against the resolution, to reaffirm both his belief in the American Way and his hostility to communism, socialism, Marxism, collectivism. Orthodoxy was thus dramatized and celebrated. That it was being menaced was perhaps obvious; yet the fact was illustrated by the appearance at Wayne State of some seventy-five students picketing to protest not the appearance of Aptheker but the fact that he had been granted an auditorium of only limited seating capacity.

This Michigan example is simply one recent of many. In the mid-1960s North Carolina's legislature enacted a statutory speaker-ban that has been a continual cause of controversy. To this extent it was a success, allowing ceaseless debate and celebration of the verities. There has been no evidence that it changed anybody's thinking at the state universities. For a number of years the Free State of Maryland has had in effect a requirement that certain speakers at state universities sign a loyalty oath before appearing. In 1965 civil rights leader Bayard Rustin, an ex-Communist, was first invited to speak at the University of Maryland and then sent a loyalty oath to sign. "I suppose," said a college official, "that if he refuses to sign it, the invitation would be cancelled." Rustin did ("As a civil libertarian I could not possibly sign any such pledge"), and the invitation was. The only measurable result of it all was a news story of some national interest.

It should be remembered that in fulfilling this function the state legislature is governed by some organic, institutional impulse. None of this implies that the members are moronic. The truth is that individual members find it extremely difficult to disassociate from the ritual. A Shriner would find it similarly difficult to insist upon asceticism and meditation at a lodge banquet. In the legislature, individuals often feel trapped by the institutional necessity. There occurred a laughable instance of this in Florida.

At Tallahassee the legislature had gotten by for generations on the assumption that the standard oath of office more or less assured the reliability of the members. Treason, in any event, was not a chronic problem. Members generally regarded their fellows as at least latent patriots.

Into this lackadaisical situation in the middle 1950s came a tall beefy realtor named Fred C. Petersen of St. Petersburg. He was elected to the house. He liked to meet head-on the central problems of society. Hence he inundated each session with legislation to ban fluoridation, ban vivisection, ban the United Nations. That sort of thing. Ninety-eight or perhaps ninety-nine per cent of Petersen's legislative program got conveniently lost in committee. As a Republican he possessed slightly less influence than a junior page, and, besides, when it came time to denounce or ban anything the legislators who ran things wanted to get the credit.

Naturally enough, Petersen began to sulk. Also, since he generally took the conspiratorial view of events, he began to wonder. He wondered whether this legislature was quite 100 per cent. This led to his crowning legislative achievement: a resolution requiring the Florida House to attest to its loyalty—not once but every day. The first time Petersen's pledge-to-the-flag resolution came up the leadership managed the pluck to send it back to committee for "further study." Petersen furrowed his brow and at length perceived that there was not really much to study about a resolution requiring a regular daily pledge to the flag. He was, of course, eminently correct here. And when he finally found the words to put the matter to the house again, in the next session, there was not sufficient pluck among the others to protest. The resolution passed. Who could oppose a daily pledge to the flag? The fact was that the house did. But the members were trapped. They abided by the resolution for days and days—ultimately repealing it by a lapse of memory.

In the Maryland legislature in 1966 came another example of how, despite a personal distaste, legislators are somehow impelled to celebrate orthodoxy. This occurred during an effort to repeal a Maryland law requiring all state employes to take a loyalty oath. The law was enacted in 1949. It was, said an advocate of repeal, Delegate Murray Abramsom of Baltimore, "born in a period of hysteria, has served whatever purpose it may have had and should be abolished. I think that it is ridiculous for free and patriotic citizens to be forced to affirm and reaffirm their loyalty." Abramson added that the law was a way of "hounding dissenters in the name of loyalty" and that it "takes on an especially ugly form in connection with schools and universities. The proliferation of tests and loyalty oaths required of teachers tends to inhibit discussion precisely where it should be most free."

There was another interesting fact. At the bill's enactment only one Maryland lawmaker had voted against it. Another sponsor of repeal said the now departed nay-sayer had been "the only man in the Maryland legislature with the guts to stand up. . . ." Now, however, in the capitol at Annapolis, there seemed to be considerable sentiment in favor of repealing the loyalty oath act. There was—but it was private. When the repealer was considered in committee the chairman was considerate enough not to put any man on record. He called for a voice vote and said: "It had better be loud and clear, because if there is any doubt, I'll have to take a roll call." With a roar that could be heard through closed doors and down the hall, the repealer was buried. Only one voice was heard shouting a lonely dissent.

Murray Abramson tried to analyze the legislative impulse that led to the act in the first place. "Loyalty," he said, "has become a cult, an obsession in the United States. But it is thought of not so much in terms of an affirmative faith for which the nation was created as in terms of stereotypes, the mere questioning of which is disloyal. Loyalty today consists of not being different or individualistic." Abramson was on the right track. To be different is to be unorthodox. The Maryland legislature was but celebrating orthodoxy.

A state legislature will not ordinarily do otherwise until some wrenching public event compels it to choose between greater and lesser verities. To hypothesize, should an innocent citizen be victimized by the operation of the Maryland law, resulting in public controversy, the legislature conceivably could be obliged to choose between American notions of fair play as they fall in conflict with the ideological orthodoxy that it has celebrated by its support of the loyalty oath law. Such a choice has not been forced on the legislature, however. Nobody has been convicted under the 1949 law.

Our century abounds with occasions on which the state legislature has fulfilled this intuitive function. Perhaps the most vivid in recent years occurred in the South in the years just following the Supreme Court's 1954 desegregation decision. Here was a frontal attack on an entire region's deepest verities, a clearly fatal blow to southern orthodoxy that nobody could mistake. At the time the behavior of the state legislatures sometimes appeared quite irrational. Not abnormal, merely irrational.

10

"THERE SIMPLY CAN BE NO
STATE RIGHT TO DEFAULT
ON A NATIONAL DUTY."
　　　　　—LeRoy Collins

When the Brown decision was handed down I was working on a paper in Fredericksburg, Virginia, an afternoon daily called the *Free Lance-Star*. From there I observed Virginia's initial response to the decision. Shortly afterward I moved to the Florida capital, Tallahassee, from which base I observed the local legislature for the *St. Petersburg Times* as well as traveling periodically to cover events in the rest of the South.

It was of course not essential to be on the scene to see that the southern state legislatures during this era appeared to be living in a fantasyland. Yet one had to be on hand to see that despite the appearance they were not actually succumbing to the fantasy.

From a distance one read only of the most preposterous legislative oratory and action. Reporters circumscribed by journalism's conventional standards of "objectivity" could not often make it clear that the legislatures did not really believe in what they were doing. One had to be very close to perceive at length that it was all an elaborate ritual, compulsively carried out.

On the day of the Brown decision in 1954 one of the visitors to the newspaper office in Fredericksburg was the local state representative, a stocky, cocky lawyer of good sense who summed up his reaction with melancholy wisdom. It was, he said regretfully, the end of an era. He knew it. I knew it. The editor knew it. Everybody knew it, everybody who gave the matter any thought at all.

Nevertheless, within a year, when the legislature at Richmond began cranking out the Massive Resistance program, this same state representative was at least as vocal as any other segregationist in an assembly full of segregationists. He seemed no longer to believe that an era had come to an end. Yet, it would outrage common sense to suppose that he did not know it. Everybody did except a few here and there who became totally alienated from reality.

This period attained an aura of true lunacy simply because southern legislatures were full of lawyers who knew reality but behaved as though they did not. In sessions that heaved and rumbled with emotion legislators trained in the law began solemnly discussing something called "interposition."

Now, here was a doctrine. Invalid at its inception and absolutely defunct since the Civil War, the doctrine was that a state could "interpose" its "sovereignty" to ward off the effects of federal law. Metaphysicians may argue a distinction between "interposition" and "nullification," but it is not worth arguing about.

Anyway, the capitols of the South in the post-Brown years rang with oratory over interposition. Firebrandmanship thrived as it had not since the days of the secessions; though entirely forensic, it was nonetheless fascinating. Alabama's legislature got off the pad fast. It interposed. It solemnly and formally declared in a resolution that the Supreme Court's desegregation decisions were "null and void."

Did this make them null and void? No.

Did Alabama believe they were null and void? No.

Did they prove to be null and void? No.

In turn, Mississippi interposed, and Virginia and South Carolina and Georgia. In Florida, the first battle in behalf of interposition was led in the house by a man who had been trained at Harvard Law School, C. Farris Bryant of Ocala, subsequently governor. "They say that interposition will do no good," he declared in the heat of battle, "but I say that it can do no harm." He was wrong there; it was harmful at least to the extent that it deceived people witless enough to believe in its efficacy.

Bryant's first effort to push through interposition failed only because the governor, acting on an obscure constitutional provision, adjourned the legislature in the middle of the debate. In the next session, however, the Florida lawmakers passed the interposition resolution. Publicly, Governor LeRoy Collins said the action "stultifies" the state. When the resolution crossed his desk he scribbled on the margin that if the measure "declaring decisions of the court to be 'null and void' is to be taken seriously, it is anarchy and rebellion against the nation. . . ." Correct.

But who took the interposition seriously? The courts? The President? The Congress? The Negro?

Finally, of course, nobody did. In the South today one may hear thoughtful people wonder why the legislatures went through such an orgy of emotion. The answer is that they were celebrating a doomed orthodoxy.

It is bootless to speculate whether it was "pointless" or not. To the innocent observer it may well seem pointless. But then so does the elaborate celebration that is called a funeral. The observer will not learn much about society by calling a funeral pointless. He may learn something by exploring why mankind has such a persisting need for this particular ritual.

This recent behavior of several of the Old South's state legislatures is deeply revealing simply because the elements are so well defined in retrospective. These instances provide illustrations of several persistent legislative characteristics.

Above all the tendency to translate the actual issue into abstract doctrine was manifest. An innocent studying the formal resolutions and documents of the period would conclude that the legislatures were defending not a policy of racial segregation but the doctrine of state sovereignty. Elaborate pupil-assignment statutes enacted during the period would reveal not a smidgen of legislative interest in race. The blunt issue of whether Negroes should be admitted to white schools was resourcefully transposed into intricate argument about ways to assign pupils to schools on the basis of "psychological needs."

Any observer will be tempted to wonder whether in all this the legislatures were not simply responding to an outcry of the people. The answer is no. Obviously the legislatures responded to the general amorphous need for a great dramatization of the collapse of a deep-seated orthodoxy. But as to the actual situation that led to it all—the segregation of the races—the legislatures invariably resisted proposals that the people be allowed to decide the question.

In Virginia, where Massive Resistance was born, there was every sign initially that the people wished to follow a sensible course. The political leadership originally formulated a program, called the Gray Plan after a state senator, that embraced the idea of local option decisions on desegregation. The plan was the culmination of a report that recognized "the varying conditions throughout the Commonwealth" and suggested "giving the greatest amount of local option to meet these conditions." The report, said one summary, "recognizes the Supreme Court decision by permitting school integration in communities that choose that course. . . ." There was a statewide vote on the plan, which amounted to a call for a constitutional convention. Results: 304,154 in favor, 144,000 against. "A substantial number," wrote Benjamin Muse, author of a history of the period called *Virginia's Massive Resistance*, "had voted for a feature of the Gray Plan which was not printed on the ballot, and which was about to be discarded: local option."

What was not generally known until later was that U.S. Senator Harry Byrd, Virginia's genial dictator for many years, had "decreed that the local option feature of the Gray Plan should be scuttled altogether," Muse noted. Subsequently, the state legislature had no intention of letting the matter get out of its hands to be settled by the people in a practical, orderly way. Other southern legislatures also adamantly rejected proposals for local option. After all, with the question in the hands of the people, the already rising ritualistic celebration of the doomed values would not even have *appeared* to have a point. As it happened, it went on for several years in Virginia and other states of the old Confederacy, accomplishing nothing.

There is yet another lesson in all this and subsequent events. It is simply that a society's need to have the passing orthodoxy celebrated does not mean that it will not accept the new. The case frequently seems to be that the people actually begin to live by the emerging standard while the state legislature celebrates the old. As a familiar if anomalous instance of this there is the case of Mississippi's prohibition of liquor. It was, in 1966, the last state in the union to maintain statewide dry laws, testimony to the fact that the creed of the orthodox teetotaler is still important to many of the numerous Protestant fundamentalists who inhabit the state. Actually, the teetotaler's creed has always been a laugh to most Mississippians. Gunnar Myrdal said he saw "more hard drinking in Mississippi" than he had ever witnessed anywhere.

Still, the legislature has regularly celebrated the old orthodoxy, assisting the growth of a subrosa liquor operation so vast that when referenda have been held the bootleggers and fundamentalists can combine in sufficient numbers to continue the prohibition, enriching the soul of the one and the pocketbook of the other.

Mississippi's current governor, Paul B. Johnson, asked the 1966 legislature to provide for another referendum and, uniquely for a Mississippi governor, Johnson put the question in such stark terms that the legislature shortly after passed a bill to let counties have legal liquor for the first time in 57 years. "A 15-year-old child," Johnson told the lawmakers, "can take a $5 bill and buy whisky in practically any county in this state. . . . Right here in Hinds County— where our Capitol is located—you can get back-door delivery for anything you want and a bill at the end of the month." Plainly the legislators already knew all this, as they have through all the years of celebrating the teetotaler's creed in a society that has never had any intention of abiding by it.

Thus in celebrating or dramatizing or defending an old orthodoxy, a legislature is not necessarily reflecting some *will* of the people. That is, it is not trying to translate actual public attitudes into practical legislation. The character of its stance is ritualistic, dramatic. Public reaffirmation of an old revered attitude is the thing. No reasonable person who has ever been there would suggest that it is the will of the people of Mississippi that liquor be banned. However, the segment of the population that reveres the notion of teetotalism is sufficiently large and respectable to elicit the conditioned legislative tribute.

Meanwhile, the institution of Law Enforcement (the police, lawyers, the courts) dramatizes the society's actual attitude toward liquor by showing patience and tolerance toward bootleggers. In this instance, the legislature functions as a custodian of the obsolete orthodoxy while the law, confronting the practical facts of daily human activity, functions as the custodian of the contemporary mores. This is not an uncommon division of roles.

New York supplies a timely example of the same thing. In this case the issue in a continuing controversy pertains not to the conditions under which one may drink liquor but the conditions under which a marriage may be dissolved.

New York's divorce law is the sternest in the nation, allowing a marriage to be terminated on only one ground, adultery. The statute was put on the books before the U. S. Constitution was adopted and for years the legislature has indulged in debates over whether to change it. Repeated arguments have always come to nothing. A major drive to write a new law occurred in the 1966 session. To the dismay of reform advocates the drive for a new law was promptly diverted by the legislative leadership, and it soon became clear that only insignificant changes could be obtained. To the sharp-eyed *New York Times* this was mystifying, as it confessed editorially late in the session. "The procedure is unusual, if not extraordinary, in this final stage," said the *Times*. "A generally good bill had been drafted by the Joint Legislative Committee after long inquiry and public hearings. This committee has now apparently lost all jurisdiction, and final revision is in the hands of the Senate Republican leader, Earl W. Brydges, the Speaker of the Assembly, Anthony J. Travia, and the chairman of the Senate Judiciary Committee, John H. Hughes. These leaders have voluntarily pre-empted a responsibility for themselves. The way in which they deliver on this self-assigned task will be watched with more than usual interest."

The way they delivered proved not substantially different from the way the New York legislature has delivered on the divorce issue at various other times in the last 179 years. Without accomplishing much, the legislature provided the stage for celebrating a fading but revered orthodoxy.

Each time this controversy arises it is an occasion for important elements in the New York society to come forward and speak about the sanctity of marriage and the necessity for preventing its disruption. These attitudes about a cherished institution are expressed with great sincerity that should not be doubted.

At the same time it is not an attitude that is shared by New Yorkers who actually desire to terminate their marriages. Marriages break up constantly for the usual reasons. Nobody cheers about this, but neither is there any more astonishment about it than in Nebraska or Maine. Marriages go bust in New York, too, and as in all such cases the notion of sanctity becomes a fiction. Divorces are obtained. Often those who want them go to Mexico or Nevada or Idaho where the laws are more amenable to practical considerations. Despite the law that is on the books, nobody is any more surprised when a New York couple gets a divorce than when the same thing happens to an Alabama couple.

Thousands of couples, however, find it for some reason expedient to obtain a divorce in New York State rather than go—as did the first Mrs. Nelson Rockefeller to divorce Nelson and the second Mrs. Rockefeller to divorce Dr. Murphy

—to the easy divorce states. Some New Yorkers, for one thing, do not have the money.

To accommodate them, however, a well-organized subrosa institution has been founded within the institution of the Law. Its operations are common knowledge and occasionally discussed in the public press, just as illicit liquor operation is common knowledge to all Mississippians.

Through New York's subrosa divorce apparatus a partner in marriage can arrange to have a private detective catch the other in—or nearly in—the act of adultery. Presto, the single acceptable ground for divorce is established. Lawyers fully aware of all this then go before courts fully aware of this, and the legal procedure is followed with unblinking solemnity. Practical and desired results are obtained in the form of binding decrees and restored maiden names and all that. In another ruse, many New York couples who wish divorces obtain them in the form of annulments simply by testifying to any one of the various grounds allowed as a basis for that legal action. The law is equally aware of this ruse, as of the fact that the state has one of the highest annulment rates in the world.

Meanwhile, the legislature celebrates the sanctity of marriage. In 1966, after protracted controversy and discussion, the New York legislature enacted a revision of the divorce law. It provided several new grounds for divorce among them mental cruelty, abandonment, imprisonment and separation for two years. Despite the tension and furor that preceded the final passage the revision slid through the senate with but a single dissenting vote. Then, after the self-congratulatory cheers died down, lawyers began to note that the actual effect of the revision would probably be slight. Because of stringent and possibly unconstitutional new residency requirements it appeared the new law would close the door to the quick Mexican divorces recently obtained by some 15,000 New Yorkers a year. Meanwhile, it would take just as long as ever to obtain a divorce in the state—two to three years. And the *New York Times* quoted one lawyer who observed that now the perjury and collusion

that had been institutionalized under the old adultery-only
statute would be brought into play to prove mental cruelty
—the usual ground for cases of incompatability. As all this
became evident one legislator drily remarked that the legislature had brought New York's divorce law out of the eighteenth century but not into the twentieth.

11

". . . THE BUSINESS OF GOV-
ERNING IS INEXTRICABLY
BOUND UP WITH THE ELAB-
ORATE AND EVER VARYING
MYTH-COMPLEX THAT LINKS
THE GOVERNORS AND THE
GOVERNED."

—R. M. MacIver,
The Web of Government

★★★★★★★★★★★★★★★★★★★
★★★★★★★★★★★★★★★★★★★

Common sense ordinarily will tell the observer when the legislature is functioning in its role as the celebrant of passé orthodoxy. However, there are several circumstances to watch for as clues.

One is the occurrence of enormous controversy simultaneously with the appearance of near unanimity. As an example, in the southern states following the Brown decision, debates of fantastic ferocity preceded the adoption of interposition resolutions by nearly unanimous votes. For another, when censorship bills are enacted, fights about their constitutionality tend to rage on and on, but few legislators dissent at final passage. Loyalty bills often give rise to this same phenomenon. Controversy amid signs of unanimity may also be noted when the legislature celebrates orthodoxy while *not* acting on a measure. For years before the 1966 revision, New York lawmakers raised great storms about the divorce law before burying revision proposals with hardly a murmur of complaint.

Another circumstance is the occurrence of an emphatic moral tone in legislative debate, an overt display of piety and virtue that tests one's credulity. It is always noticeable because it is always incongruous. Lawmakers who are known to spend their happiest moments grappling for some matron's garter belt tend to emerge as voluble champions of enforced universal chastity. Similarly, statehouse reporters learn to watch for the lawmaker with the cesspool mind to join the front lines of any battle to take smut off the newsstands.

It is the shrill moralizing that drives dissent into the hole during such celebrations. At the end, the dissenter is invariably made to appear to be in favor of polygamy or alcoholism or treason or dirty words.

The third circumstance to watch for is the probability that the legislative controversy, whatever its conclusion, will have no substantial bearing on the events of actual life. To illustrate, if the legislature climaxes an ideological celebration by enacting some kind of loyalty statute, it will result in neither more loyalty nor less than if the statute had not been enacted. Similarly, when the legislature passes a stronger censorship bill in salute to certain attitudes about wholesome literature, fanciers of smut need never fear that the supply will be cut off or diminished. It never is.

Legislatures know this when they enact such laws. The relevancy of such laws to actual life has no bearing on the legislature's action. It is celebrating some faded orthodoxy.

This variety of action, however, frequently results in some damage to the public psyche, and it may cause some inconvenience. But it seldom has a substantial effect on the way life goes. Burned-out marriages have continued to end in divorce in New York, and, in Mississippi, no thirst has ever gone unslaked for lack of liquor. There occurred another example in Albany in 1965: the legislature staged a lengthy debate over whether to repeal the law defining adultery as a crime. After much ennobling oratory, the lawmakers voted overwhelmingly that adultery *should* be considered a crime. Thus nothing was changed. Nor was there the slightest belief that the frequency of adultery would be affected by the fact that the legislature now had elaborately and noisily declared it still to be a crime.

The foregoing does not mean that legislative behavior in celebration of orthodoxy does not sometimes substantially affect the lives of a few individuals. Indeed, when this legislative predilection gives rise to the witch-hunt syndrome or the thought-control syndrome one corroborating sign of it is evidence that the *only* thing the legislature will accomplish is to victimize some individual or perhaps several.

Such, for example, was the nature and result of action taken by the Georgia House in 1966 in the Julian Bond case. Bond was a twenty-six-year-old Negro, a leader of the civil rights organization called the Student Nonviolent Coordinating Committee. He was properly elected to the Georgia House and was scheduled to be sworn in along with a handful of other new Negro members. The house, however, refused to seat Bond.

The case against him was that statements he had made disapproving of American policy in Vietnam proved his philosophy incompatible with the U.S. Constitution. It is not even necessary to see the absurdity of this to understand that the Georgia house was only celebrating orthodoxy on several different levels at once. It was dramatizing the traditional American attitude that every citizen, even at the cost of free speech, must support the nation when it is at war. It was dramatizing the orthodox white Georgian attitude toward civil rights agitators. It was, finally, celebrating its own orthodox but now defunct notion that the governing body of the state should be lily white.

The only thing the Georgia house accomplished, however, was to make a victim of Julian Bond. Indirectly, of course, it also assured that Bond's views would receive far more attention than they would have otherwise. However, there was no indication that the house advanced the Vietnam war effort or helped unite the American people behind the Administration. Certainly the house action did not establish any new legislative policy: after spending years thwarting Washington's efforts to obtain constitutional equality for the Negro, white Georgia lawmakers were not suddenly taking the view that the national government had to be supported in *all* its quests. War was merely hell; total integration had been unthinkable. All the Georgia House was doing was celebrating orthodoxy with a one-shot witch hunt.

Because of prevalent preconceptions about the Old South, and because its racial troubles have dominated the news of the recent decade, the observer may be tempted to assume that the legislative characteristics under discussion are more typical of the southern state legislature. The temptation should be resisted, the assumption rejected.

An almost compulsive predilection for orthodoxy is an institutional characteristic that sporadically manifests itself in every state legislature. It does not result merely when (as in the South) a homogenous society confronts the rupture of ancient, deep-rooted tradition. Is is not a result of legislative control by rural elements or by ignorant and unsophisticated elements. Students of this subject could argue, in fact, that nowhere has this legislative characteristic been manifested so virulently and persistently as in New York for the last fifty years and California for the last twenty.

The observer may find a brief elaboration here useful, simply because New York is regarded by many Americans as the nation's most "sophisticated" state; and California, in turn, as the census figures show, has grown so fast that its society has no deep-rooted pervasive "traditions" except those that are pasted together from time to time by state publicists. First, some notes on New York.

"No other state," wrote Columbia College Dean Lawrence H. Chamberlain, "has shown so continuous a sense of insecurity." He documented the observation in a book called *Loyalty and Legislative Action—A Survey of Activity by the New York State Legislature 1919–1949.*

Chamberlain tells the history of the so-called Lusk investigation. It began in 1919, the crusade of a legislative committee created in March of that year and headed by Senator Clayton Lusk, a Cortland, N.Y., lawyer who had only been a legislator since January. This was a period, of course, when orthodox American economic notions appeared to be menaced both by socialist dogma and by labor's heightened efforts to obtain leverage in the capitalist system. One teacher suspected of promoting Bolshevist doctrine had been suspended from Commercial High School in

New York City. The mission of the Lusk committee was, ostensibly, to see how much of this sort of thinking was going on.

It plunged into its task by raiding the headquarters of a variety of radical organizations (the American Civil Liberties Union among them) through 1919 and 1920. On November 8, 1919, the committee raided about seventy "Red centers" in New York City. It seized tons of literature and arrested more than a thousand persons.

"It seems to me," said Lusk, "that the time has come to put into force stern measures to do away with this agitation. . . ." His committee appeared to be doing its best. Chamberlain noted that it tended to burn the subversive stamp on every program and viewpoint with which it disagreed. It tended to castigate pacifists, liberals and those who simply disagreed with the committee's methods and goals. "This lack of discrimination," said Chamberlain, "is the more reprehensible because of the committee's habitual practice of dragging in the names of persons upon the least pretext. The technique of smear by slanting innuendo runs through almost every public statement."

The key bills of several that the Lusk committee promoted in the legislature provided stringent licensing measures for teachers and required them to prove, among other things, that they were "in hearty accord and sympathy with the government and institutions of the state of New York and of the United States." After an enormous amount of discussion the legislature passed them with near unanimity (43–8 in the senate and with only three negative votes in the assembly). Then the bills encountered Governor Alfred Smith's veto.

"It is unthinkable," said Smith, "that in a representative democracy there should be delegated to any body of men the absolute power to prohibit the teaching of any subject of which it may disapprove."

Governor Nathan L. Miller evidently did not agree. He signed the bills after the legislature repassed them in 1920. Then, in 1923, after an enormous amount of discussion, the legislature repealed them.

In his detailed study, Dean Chamberlain relates the background of the Ives Loyalty Oath Law, named for Assembly Majority Leader (later U.S. Senator) Irving M. Ives, who introduced it in 1934 as an antidote to "too much teaching of various 'isms' in the schools." It was passed, vetoed, then passed again slightly amended.

The 1936 New York legislature also entertained a bill to put the American flag into every classroom. It passed the New York Senate, 48–2, after Senator Joe R. Hanley declared: "We want people to respect the flag and if they will not respect it voluntarily, then we will make them respect it involuntarily." The bill was later amended to require the flag only in every school assembly hall.

In the late 1930s, with orthodoxy still in a period of marked transition, there was another Lusk-like investigation, led by Senator John J. McNaboe of New York City, into "hotbeds of communism" among students and teachers in New York schools. In 1939 McNaboe sponsored a bill designed to bar Communists from civil service but defined "Communist" in such broad terms that even the New York League of Women Voters attacked the measure. This led to a slightly less objectionable bill that bore the name of another sponsor.

All this proved only a prelude to the so-called Rapp-Coudert investigations of 1940–41—the fruit of a legislative resolution triggered by the news that Bertrand Russell had been appointed professor of philosophy at City College. As Chamberlain noted, the legislature disapproved Russell's views on "the conventional canons of morality, particularly the institution of marriage." Senator Herbert A. Rapp lent his name to the subsequent legislative action with a resolution calling for an investigation of school financing problems. After the unsettling news about Russell's appointment, the resolution was broadened to include subversive activities among the school deficiencies to be explored. Senator Frederic R. Coudert, Jr., of New York City became vice chairman of the investigating committee.

Now, despite all of this diligence, by 1949 the New York legislature still acted as though it were uneasy about subversives in the public school system. It passed the Feinberg law, named for the senate majority leader. This law strengthened the existing statute that already provided: "A person employed as superintendent of schools, teacher or employe in the public schools of the state shall be removed for the utterance of any treasonable or seditious word or words or the doing of any treasonable or seditious act or acts while holding such position."

Details of the statutes that resulted from this activity are not essential to understanding what the legislature was actually doing. None of this had any substantial impact on the course of events. It had only the result of leaving behind numbers of victims. Some persons were damaged in hearings and speeches. There were others. In 1920, while the Lusk committee was still conducting sorties on various radical organizations, the New York Assembly voted, 140 to 6, to refuse to seat five duly elected members. They happened to be socialists.

"The five men," Chamberlain recorded, "were herded before the speaker's rostrum like pickpockets before a police magistrate and were informed that they had been elected on a platform inimical to the best interests of the state and nation." Then, *after six weeks of hearings*, the assembly kicked them out—by overwhelming majorities.

Charity and tolerance were the virtues of Chamberlain's final reflections upon these events. He decided to write off the Lusk investigation "as a perversion" because, "one does not appraise an institution or process upon the basis of the most degenerate sample." Then he applied "something of the same order of logic" to the McNaboe investigation. Having done this he found the Rapp-Coudert investigation "all the more disturbing." After all, led by decent men, it had "none of the hypocrisy or the buffoonery of its two predecessors." Yet the Rapp-Coudert probe did produce "unnecessary personal hardship and mental anxiety." Ultimately, Chamberlain concluded, the New York experience "suggests that whenever subversive activity becomes the subject of investigation by a politically constituted committee it is difficult to prevent injustices from occurring or innocent persons from being injured."

Chamberlain's delicacy of judgment reflects a wistful reluctance to cut through to a fundamental truth. "The veneration we rightly feel for the Constitution," as Rickover observed, "makes exploration in depth of our political system seem almost sacrilegious."

Thus Chamberlain writes off the Lusk investigation as "a perversion" by which the institution should not be judged. Then he applies the "same order of logic" to the McNaboe investigation. Further, he finds the character of the Rapp-Coudert investigation all the more disquieting simply because Rapp and Coudert were "persons of integrity."

What Chamberlain has not perceived, evidently, is that an individual in the legislature tends to behave not according to his own norms but according to the impulses of the institution of which he has become a part. Chamberlain is properly enough perturbed that the investigation by the honorable Messrs. Rapp and Coudert "produced unnecessary personal hardship and anxiety." He would have been less astonished at this result if he had come to recognize that such is the unfailing result—the establishment of victims—when the legislature's obsessive attention to orthodoxy is manifested in the witch-hunt syndrome.

At one point in his summary, Dean Chamberlain did nearly come to final terms with this characteristic of the witch hunt: "A committee set up to study subversive activity," he says, "cannot resist the temptation to unearth 'subversives.' "

This point was put more intriguingly once by Carey McWilliams, the editor of *Nation*, in his book called *Witch Hunt*. "Witches are not made or spawned or fashioned; they are caught," he wrote. "Hunting witches is like playing a game: the witch is the one at whom the others point. Without a witch hunt, there would be no witches, and witches are never hunted without a reason. Witch hunts are a means by which, in time of storm, the belief in witches is exploited in order to control men's thoughts and to police their loyalties."

There is one further characteristic of the witch hunt. Witches are always caught. To a state legislature the witch is commonly a person who dramatizes his opposition to the prevailing or passing orthodoxy. In New York in 1920 the witches were, among others, five men who won election to the legislature while calling themselves socialists. This had nothing to do with their loyalty to the country. In 1966 in Georgia the witch was a Negro pacifist named Julian Bond.

It is obvious, of course, to most reasonable men, that one can express one's loyalty to one's country through pacifism as well as through belligerence. In these instances, however, the state legislature is not actually concerned with loyalty to the nation or loyalty to the state. It is concerned with adherence to orthodoxy. More accurately still, it is concerned that the contemporary orthodoxy is crumbling or profoundly challenged.

At such times, without a signal, the legislature stages celebrations and dramatizations of the old orthodoxy. In 1949 Benjamin Fine, the *New York Times'* former education editor, reported that educators were "alarmed and dismayed" that Kansas, Massachusetts and Pennsylvania had passed acts providing for the firing of teachers for "disloyalty"—and that Maryland, New York and New Jersey had adopted laws forbidding teachers to join certain organizations, that a score of states had authorized loyalty checkups on nonteaching school employes.

By now the observer should begin to realize that the New York legislative activity Chamberlain felt constrained to write off as a "perversion" is in fact a common and universal manifestation of the state legislative character. "Why has New York," Chamberlain asked, "been so obsessed with the specter of disloyalty?" A half-answer is that New York has not been *uniquely* obsessed.

In California in 1949 the legislature had pending at one

time at least fifteen thought-control bills that would have required loyalty oaths from lawyers, teachers, state employes—and members of the state legislature. The fruit of much investigating by the state's un-American activities committee under the chairmanship of Senator Jack B. Tenney, these bills eventually were tabled—but not without an enormous amount of debate and not before their mere existence had helped precipitate the notorious loyalty oath crisis that wracked the faculty of the University of California at Berkeley. McWilliams wrote of all this in *Witch Hunt*.

In nearly all efforts to account for state legislative behavior of this sort commentators are almost always content to settle for proximate causes, the triggering conditions. In writing against New York's Lusk laws, however, John Dewey went deeper. They were, he said, "only the *outward symbol* of that tendency on the part of big business in our present economic society to hold teachers within definite prescribed limits. These suppressive tendencies work in a more refined way than laws. The great body of teachers are unaware of their existence. They are felt only through little hints about 'safety,' 'sanity,' and 'sobriety' coming from influential sources. . . . It is something more than academic freedom that is being menaced. It is moral freedom, the right to think, to imagine. It involves, when it is crushed, a crushing of all that is best in the way of inspiration and ideals for a better order."

Even Dewey's penetrating insight left the actual legislative role not fully illuminated. It is true that the New York legislature in 1919–1920 was triggered into its peculiar activity because the orthodox economic notions of the time appeared to be endangered by alien dogma. But the observer will obtain a fuller appreciation of the institutional dynamics of that legislative response if he goes on to reflect that in the 1960s the American legislature is still regularly celebrating those old economic notions long after they have been discarded in the actual practices of the American system by whatever label it is described.

12

★★★★★★★★★★★★★★★★★★★★
★★★★★★★★★★★★★★★★★★★★

"NO ADEQUATE STUDY OF
TWENTIETH-CENTURY CAPI-
TALISM EXISTS. SCHOLARLY
COMMENTATORS ARE QUITE
AWARE THAT THE DESCRIP-
TIVE CLICHES STILL IN CUR-
RENT USE ARE LITTLE MORE
THAN A DEPOSIT OF VERBI-
AGE LEFT OVER FROM A PRE-
VIOUS HISTORICAL AGE."

—Adolf A. Berle, Jr.,
*The 20th Century
Capitalist Revolution*

★★★★★★★★★★★★★★★★★★★★
★★★★★★★★★★★★★★★★★★★★

I am aware that I ask the ob-
server to examine the state legislature in an unaccustomed
way. I suggest, briefly, that social practices change but
that society still needs to have the old beliefs and mores and
doctrines celebrated and dramatized, and that the state
legislature responds and fills this need.

On reflection anyone will realize it is not unusual for
institutions so to function. The monarchy in England functions as the celebrant of notions and ideas long since defunct. The House of Lords exists for practically no other
purpose. In America and elsewhere the church is the reposi-
tory for moral ideals that are not used in day-to-day life but
are trotted out and celebrated on Sundays or feast days or
holidays. In the courts from time to time we see dramatized
ethical notions of far greater purity than those in actual use.
Every time someone is sent away on an income tax charge
millions upon millions of Americans shudder and brood
upon their own actual propensities.

In spite of all this it is still at first jolting to conceive of the state legislature's comparable institutional functions. Our habits of thought are deep and abiding. We tend to think of the legislature in terms of its constitutional functions, its statutory functions: it passes laws, it taxes, it appropriates, it builds roads, it finances colleges, it creates judgeships, it creates and abolishes municipalities, it writes the penal code. Or we tend to think of it in terms of those wispy but powerful sentiments that are the stuff of our political spirituality. "Although the executive and judiciary are elected by the people and are answerable to them," wrote political reporter Hugh Morris in the *Louisville Courier-Journal* as Kentucky opened its 1966 session, "only the legislature is truly 'the people's branch' of state government. In the collective hands of the 138 locally elected legislators reposes the full sovereignty of the state and its people." When not thus shrouding them in abstractions, our habit at other times is to think of the legislature in terms of specific issues (Will the teachers get a pay raise?) or in terms of party politics (Now that the Democrats are in control, what will they do?).

Mostly, of course, we do not think at all about the state legislature. We the People do not have much interest in it. Political preachers are forever telling us that we ought to have more, but this does not alter the public indifference that is well documented in a variety of ways—including studies of participation in legislative elections, and in referenda on state constitutional reforms. We are told repeatedly that if we were more interested that state government would be better. Still, we are not much interested. I have realized increasingly that one thing I am trying to do in these comments is explain why we are not interested.

To say that state government (the state legislature) seems to have no vital relevancy to our lives is, of course, but another way of stating disinterest. Ultimately, to fathom the reason for it, one must first comprehend the state legislature as an institution and comprehend further that it has for a long long time been the custodian of obsolescent notions, ones that plain observation demonstrates no longer have any vital relevancy to our day-to-day lives. The state legislature clings to and celebrates these notions not as a reflection of the will of the people but in answer to some unarticulated need of the society. For instance, in the 1930s when FDR was leading the nation through a period of radical change in national economic and political policy, nearly every legislature responded to the trend by repeatedly and emotionally celebrating the old doctrine and policies—while the people overwhelmingly registered their approval of the new. A whole series of national elections stands as evidence of this. Eventually, of course, even the commercial and corporate community discarded nearly all the active hostility that it felt toward the new ways and today follows practices that dramatize actual complete acceptance. Were it otherwise, then in 1964 Barry Goldwater might have carried more than five states, and Lyndon Johnson, advocate of policies more "radical" than FDR's, probably would have carried fewer than forty-five.

All this leads back to the point that in spite of the actualities of the day the state legislature in the 1960s is still celebrating not merely the old eroded ideological doctrine but economic doctrine that has been obsolete lo these many years. The state legislature does this, moreover, despite the fact that its individual members, as lawyers and businessmen, have long since discarded the old notions in their own personal and commercial lives.

So doggedly does the legislature cling to the outmoded notions that intelligent up-to-date financial experts do not often like to become involved with the state capitol operations. In one recent National Municipal League pamphlet New York Senate Secretary Albert J. Abrams put it this way: "[Budget-making] research that is limited to compiling routine data and summary of existing thinking on problems, *a characteristic of much legislative research today* [my emphasis] is not capable of attracting the best minds." Further, what Abrams calls the legislature's *existing thinking* is not what Galbraith would call the *conventional wis-*

dom of today. It is the conventional wisdom of deceased generations.

(I would have appropriated Galbraith's phrase for more use in these comments but for the fact that *wisdom* connotes a quality I do not wish to suggest when I use a phrase like the conventional lore or the passing orthodoxy. I prefer these as a catchall descriptive of society's notions and attitudes, the doctrine and theory and values that are held rigidly if impermanently at a given time. There is a certain arbitrariness about all transient conventional attitudes. To speak of the conventional *wisdom* is to hint at a rationality that I am not persuaded is there in our economic or social doctrine.)

Anyway, whether it is to be called the existing thinking or the conventional wisdom or obsolescent orthodoxy the economic ways of the state legislature are far removed from those of the rest of the American society.

A secluded Tibetan monk, if he had been forced to observe America only through the words and behavior of the state legislature, would have concluded that this nation had suffered from unrelieved depression throughout the two decades since World War II.

Every American knows, to the contrary, that these have been times of unparalleled prosperity. Nonetheless, the impression of incipient economic collapse has been created in each state capitol, as even a casual newspaper reader must be aware. Even in the rosiest of times the state legislature manages to generate the aura of financial stress. A headline from the *Wall Street Journal* of August 17, 1965, illustrates the point:

Surprise Surpluses
State Tax Collections
Soar Above Estimates,
Easing Fiscal Squeeze

Sharp Revenue Rise, Credited
To Business Boom, Helps
Some Avoid Tax Increases

―――――

But Crisis Warnings Remain

The observer is invited to note, primarily, that, despite rising revenues and a business boom, *crisis warnings remain*. To this extent the *Journal* headline accurately reflects an impression that is created in nearly every state capitol in nearly every session.

This is not merely a symptom of the *Journal's* editorial antipathy to governmental spending. With few exceptions, every state legislature throughout this period of unprecedented prosperity has perennially or biennially behaved as though the country were teetering close to poverty.

An individual who so behaves is put down as an eccentric in the society. When, following a life of ostentatious deprivation, he dies and leaves a large sum of money, the newspapers write feature stories about him and readers speculate on the notions that governed his behavior. It appears irrational at worst, impractical at best. One thing that can be agreed upon is that in such instances the governing notions were obsessive or compulsive or, in the language of some clinicians, obsessive-compulsive. Similarly, the state legislature often appears to be governed by a set of obsessive economic notions.

They are, to be sure, familiar notions, still cherished by the people even though they are no longer used in day-to-day life. They are, by and large, the economic notions of the eighteenth and nineteenth centuries and may be distilled into several words and slogans. One of these governing ideas is the notion of thrift as a virtue. There is a companion notion relating to indebtedness.

Beyond doubt these notions lie deep in the American creed. They were practiced for many years. Benjamin Franklin preached thrift unremittingly, and cash-on-the-barrelhead was part of both the language and the fiscal theology of the country. The pinch-penny attitude of John D. Rockefeller became a national legend; even when he was gouging millions out of his fellows he concerned himself with what one of his barrel factories had done with 500 missing bungs worth a few cents each. The former prevalence of the notion of thrift in American life is obvious, as is the fact that to be in debt was long regarded as a bad thing.

Yet it must be plain to even a casual spectator at the American scene that these notions about thrift and indebtedness no longer prevail. They are cherished but obsolete. Parents still cite Benjamin Franklin to their children while living in a house owned by a bank or mortgage company and furnished with appliances bought on the installment plan. In the spring of 1966 CBS television tried to sum up America's individual debts in a show whose title revealed its conclusion. "I.O.U. $315,000,000,000," it was called. Politicians continue to feign great concern over the government's national debt; yet if any one of them seriously proposed eliminating it he would be regarded as a nut, a demagogue, a fool or all three.

One of the most traditional and conservative elements in our society is the banking industry, which, as anyone must notice, works harder these days persuading people to borrow than encouraging people to save. By its very nature the corporate world would collapse if it were not for borrowed money, and, although corporate executives are still obliged to preach thrift from time to time, they actually live like princes on extravagant expense accounts. The notion of thrift is so cherished, however, that a man is thought to be somehow unsound if he does not express sympathy with it. On the other hand, an executive who purports to practice it in fact is often ill-regarded and may even cause his company to suffer a loss of confidence. Every corporation headquarters is familiar with the executive who returns from a $41.75 lunch (or a $1,218.25 trip to a policy conference in the Bahamas) and decides that his subordinates have been spending too much money on, say, telephone calls. If the martinis or holiday have sufficiently dulled his wits he may actually put out a memorandum demanding a reduction in this waste. If he does, of course, his staff will suffer a prompt loss of morale that will reflect itself in decreased production until the economy or thrift memorandum is forgotten. Ordinarily this takes thirty-six to forty-eight hours.

Without having to put it into words, Americans know that if the country suddenly started practicing thrift and living by the old cash-and-carry creed the economy would collapse overnight. Yet these notions are revered, and a social need to have them celebrated seems to persist. This need appears to be fulfilled by the state legislature.

It is the last institution in American society that still pretends to be operating according to the old creed of thrift. (Lyndon Johnson's attention to turning off the White House lights is a touch of quaintness that hardly disguises the dimensions of his programs and budgets.) The banks don't, nor do the savings-and-loan companies. Loan sharks, legalized and euphemized under the label small-loan companies, keep the airwaves crackling with their jingles and commercials urging the hard-pressed to solve their problems by quick borrowing. *"Ben-e-fi-cial Fi-nance is the one place to go . . . for mon-ey the min-ute you want it."* The building industry would have stagnated long since without a harvest of U.S. guaranteed loans to individuals, and without the eagerness of credit companies the automobile industry would sputter to a halt. Airlines beg potential travelers to take their vacations on credit, and the staggering variety of easily obtainable credit cards is part of our folklore already.

It is not necessary to approve these facts of life, but one should acknowledge them. The observer conscious of these real conditions will more likely perceive that the economic behavior of the state legislature is singular in American society. It alone regularly celebrates the notion of thrift, the virtue of debtlessness. This accounts for the fact that the illusion of a fiscal crisis is created year after year in every American state capitol.

Obviously, without the appearance of financial stress as a backdrop, the legislative dramatization of thrift would lack verisimilitude. Thus it is that one predictable prelude to a session is the setting of the stage for the institutional ceremonials that will follow.

13

" 'WHERE DO YOU THINK WE WILL GET THE MONEY?' I ASKED. . . . 'FROM TAXES!' THE AUDIENCE BROKE OUT IN THE BEST APPLAUSE I HAD HEARD."

—Ex-North Carolina Governor Terry Sanford, *But What About the People?*

★★★★★★★★★★★★★★★★★★★
★★★★★★★★★★★★★★★★★★★

One encounters citizens who suppose that the appearance of chronic financial difficulties is a phenomenon peculiar to the state in which they live. It is, however, a phenomenon that occurs in every state.

This is a near constant. It does not seem to be subject to much variation. The creation of an appearance of financial stress coincides with the meeting of the state legislature wherever it convenes, whether in rich New York or half-rich Mississippi, whether in idyllic Hawaii or arctic Alaska, in dwindling Arkansas or in burgeoning California. It occurs year after year, biennium after biennium.

This phenomenon, it should be emphasized, is the *appearance* of financial stress, not the actuality. In the recent booming decades the states have not been in a condition of chronic fiscal crisis; the chronic condition has been that of the state legislature.

With immense resources at hand, the state legislature has continued to behave as though money were tight, an illusion that can be demolished with whole libraries full of documentation. The state legislature in this regard is governed not by the actuality of the general prosperity but by obsolete economic notions. To make the expression of these notions seem valid, it is necessary to make them seem practical. Since a pinch-penny attitude toward public improvements makes no sense in a time of abundance, the state legislature spends much time and energy making it seem that conditions of scarcity exist.

One could hardly select a better period than the mid-1960s to observe this behavior. And it is fitting to observe briefly through the eyes of the *Wall Street Journal*. One can be all but certain that the *Journal* is not sneakily advancing any radical whims about government's role in society.

Anyway, under the headline quoted earlier ("State Tax Collections Soar . . . But Crisis Warnings Remain"), the *Journal* reported:

> That traditional fiscal weakling, the state treasury, is looking surprisingly robust these days—thanks in no small measure to the curative effects of a four-year business boom.

> So high have state tax collections been running this year that state after state reports it is in the best fiscal shape in a long time. Indeed, projected deficits are being transformed into unaccustomed surpluses so rapidly as *to make persistent past warnings of impending state fiscal crisis seem, at best, considerably exaggerated—and in some cases, perhaps, like a case of crying wolf. The warnings haven't faded away entirely.* [My emphasis.]

What the *Journal* went on to detail was that many states were accumulating far more money than anticipated —$122 million in Michigan, $91 million in Pennsylvania, $44 million in Florida, $100 million in Illinois, $35.9 million in Wisconsin, $108 million in Texas—to name just some. These were amounts left over at the end of a fiscal year, amounts of money beyond legislative appropriations.

Such an amount is called a "surplus," and this nomenclature itself may be revealing to one who takes the trouble to catalogue various public institutions and programs that need money. This, in any event, was in mid-1965, and it is not my purpose to belabor any state legislature for failing to

predict exactly what existing state taxes would produce.
The administrative side of government is ordinarily liable
for this variety of failure, an excusable one.

Still, there are other things that the observer should
note. One is that in the legislative sessions prior to the development of these "surpluses" an aura of fiscal crisis did
obtain. Moreover, even after it had become clear that this
was a bountiful year, the aura of fiscal crisis did not disap-
pear from the legislative scene. It would not have been in
character for the state legislature to sit down like the
Houyhnhnms and decide which previously neglected public
improvements and programs to invest the money in.

It was in character for the states to fan up more intima-
tions of crisis. "Most states," reported the *Journal,* "regard
their current prosperity as a momentary thing, and expect
rising costs and citizen demands for more and more services
to land them back in the financial soup again before long."

Maryland was one of many states that carried such a
surplus into 1966. It totaled $27.5 million. At Annapolis, as
the general assembly convened, Governor J. Millard Tawes
proposed budgeting it. He did not propose raising taxes.
There was scarcely a socialistic innovation in the programs
to be financed. The reaction to his budget was more or less
typical.

Lawmakers promptly accused him of "fiscal brinkman-
ship." Assemblyman J. Glenn Beall, Jr., turned to traditional metaphor: "It is hypocrisy to deplete the rainy day
fund when the sun is shining bright on Maryland," he said.
"There must be places in the budget where we can cut," said
Senator Edward T. Hall.

Just so, a "surplus" became not a cause for relaxing
fiscal tensions but simply a new trigger for the expression of
the same old legislative anxieties. Frontier frugality must be
celebrated, even when the treasury appears to be running
over.

The ultimate object of the state legislature, to repeat, is
to justify the appearance of scrimping in appropriating for
public programs. Its celebration of thrift ultimately takes

this form. It is to lend the appearance of reasonableness to the scrimping that the aura of financial stress is engendered. In the usual course of events the governor of a state plays a supporting role in the drama by which the crisis is established. The drama follows a plot as predictable as a horse opera.

(A) The governor proposes a budget. (B) The legislature says that it would bankrupt the state. (C) Thrift is celebrated in committee hearings, floor debate and "behind-the-scenes" maneuvering. Stories appear in the press about an "economy bloc" of "tightfisted" lawmakers bearing "paring knives" to "whittle down the budget" or "turning on the heat" to "boil out the fat" so that a "giveaway" philosophy of "tax-tax-tax, spend-spend-spend" will not prevail. Et cetera. (D) Legislature approves budget within a few percentage points of governor's proposal after adjusting it to logrolling schemes perfected in conference committee.

No matter what state he calls home, the observer should recognize the essential accuracy of this sequence of events. When new taxes are to be enacted the celebration of thrift is accompanied by a corollary dramatization of the old cash-and-carry or pay-as-you-go principle. Some practical politicians might tend, in fact, to view the celebration of thrift as a more or less conscious effort on the part of the legislature to prepare the way for new taxes. An equally practical interpretation is that the celebration of thrift is a way of resisting new taxes. Whatever the use to which it is turned, the celebration varies little.

It always begins when the governor proposes a budget. It is always a *record* budget. This is the most natural thing in the world, yet much is made of the fact by state politicians, hence by newsmen who cover their activities and attitudes. Sample news items from the 1966 openings:

From the *New York Times*: "Trenton, Jan. 11—Gov. Richard J. Hughes appeared before the 190th session of the Legislature after it convened today and put forth the *most ambitious and expensive program* for government in the state's history."

From the *Los Angeles Times* of February 10: "Sacramento—Exact figures of governmental spending proposed for the coming year were disclosed Wednesday when Gov. Brown formally submitted his *record* $4,606,838,333 budget to the Legislature."

From the *Washington Star* of January 19: "Annapolis —The Maryland General Assembly convened today and received a *record* $883 million operating budget that requires no tax rise but hints at an increase next year."

From the *Washington Post* of January 14: "Richmond —The outgoing Harrison administration today presented details of its $2.2 billion budget for the next two years, revealing a *massive investment* in education and *setting the stage* for debate over major fiscal changes in Virginia. . . . Buoyed by a 'surprise' $96-million surplus, the *record* budget nevertheless anticipates a statewide sales tax starting at 2 per cent this September will be needed to make ends meet."

From the *New York Times*: "Albany, Jan. 18—Governor Rockefeller sent a budget marked down slightly below $4 billion to the Legislature today. The Governor proposed a *record* program of $3.98-billion, with spending pared just enough to avoid having to submit the state's first $4 billion budget in an election year."

With minor variations, it always begins thus. The simple, inevitable fact that the budget is bigger than ever carries its own implication of fiscal strain, an implication that is magnified by the conventions of daily news reporting, and which the governor conventionally attempts to counteract by applauding his own prudence. "Strict economy," said Maryland's Tawes of his budget. "Financially sound and socially responsible," said Rockefeller of his.

Invariably, by humanitarian standards, the governor's budget is something more than prudent. Though naturally larger than the previous one, it is always smaller than needed. One has yet to hear of a proposed budget sufficiently generous to eliminate crowded classrooms, for instance, while fulfilling such other demonstrable needs as decent teacher salaries, excellent care for the mentally ill, and the elimination of that plethora of civil plagues associated with the plight of the cities. One encounters governors who might agree that it would be good, even wise, to do these things. But one does not encounter governors who propose to do so. The country's governors are consistently conservative. They have to be. They must deal with the state legislature.

Even a modest budget, every governor knows, may well be treated by the legislature as though it reeked of bolshevism. When New Jersey's Hughes presented his $900-million program to the 1966 session, Senator Thomas J. Hillery, as the *Times* reported it, turned to a colleague and muttered: "This isn't a program, it's the birth of a nation." In Michigan, Governor George Romney unfurled a budget of about $900 million, prompting Senate Appropriations Chairman Garland Lane to uncork the old "giveaway" epithet. "I'm concerned with the philosophy that we've got to give away everything," said Lane. Down the hall in Lansing Representative Arnell Engstrom pointed ominously to some elusive "line between responsible progress and dangerous excesses." Presumably a general solution of all Michigan's public problems would be an unthinkably dangerous excess. This was not proposed in Romney's budget, however. In Romney's legislature there were moments when it was difficult to remember that at this time, 1966, Michigan expected a surplus not of $122 million as the *Wall Street Journal* had reported the previous year, but of $136 million.

Governors themselves, of course, often resort to the language of fiscal crisis. Their purpose, however, is usually distinguishable from that of the state legislature. It is the legislature's seldom varying purpose to create the impression that the state is nearly at the end of its resources: we have gone as far as we can go; there is nothing left to tax; the people will not stand for more taxes. It is a phantasmal vista of insolvency to which the legislature alarmingly points.

The governor is in a position to know better. At any

rate, when he employs the language of fiscal crisis he does not commonly suggest that the state has nowhere to turn for money. On the contrary, he often advances specific suggestions. He asks, in short, for additional taxes. His purpose is to shake and goad the legislature into action, while the legislative purpose is to avoid action. The legislature intimates that the fiscal stress prohibits action or warns of fiscal crisis *if* it acts. The governor, on the other hand, usually warns that crisis will result if the legislature does *not* act.

Perhaps I seem to belabor the distinction. Still, one must perceive the critical difference between the gubernatorial state of mind and the legislative. To the casual observer they often seem to be talking about the same fiscal crisis, and where this confusion occurs gubernatorial orations have lent an undue validity to the contemporary lore on this subject. For the most part, however, the governor—partly because of the nature of his office, partly because of the constituency to which he responds—fashions an estimate of the fiscal situation by projecting needs and surveying resources. Crisis thus appears imminent to him only if the state does not tap its resources deeply enough to meet the needs. To this extent the crisis of which the governor speaks exists in reality. On the other side, the state legislature engenders an aura of crisis not by juxtaposing needs and resources but by promoting the notion that the state is short on resources, or that it will cause great distress to tap them. To this extent the crisis of which the legislature speaks is a fabrication.

Who can but marvel at the proposition that the states—particularly in the last two decades—have lacked abundant economic resources? The prospering society has had no trouble whatever providing the money needed for a plethora of national programs. In 1965 the government in Washington even found it expedient temporarily to shut off some sources of revenue despite a growing number of programs to finance. Even with those pockets of poverty due to uneven distribution of prosperity, the nation has been rich enough to send billions overseas and still leave plenty of money in the pocket. Corporation profits have been fantastic, and the big decisions confronting the great middle class have been not whether to get a new car but when, not whether to get a TV for the children's room but whether to get color. Miami Beach's posh hotels have suffered only when the high-living American has decided to go the Bahamas that season, or Europe, California, Mexico. The state legislature yet has advanced the proposition that the prospering people and booming economy that existed in the nation somehow did not exist in the states. The truth is that no state, including the poorest, has even scratched its resources much less strained them.

This is not likely to change markedly in the future—simply because of the political character that the nation has assumed. The avenues of action open to the state legislature now are somewhat limited, not by any restrictions or constrictions inherent in the state government but by the pervasive disenchantment and distrust of the people. If they should choose to function through the state, obviously the people still have unlimited power. At the hands of the state legislature, however, they have experienced a history of disappointment. Because of this they have long since diverted many of their wishes for social betterment—and much of their power—into other channels. The degree of the people's alienation from the state legislature—or of the legislature from the people—will be explored later. Meanwhile, back briefly to the "fiscal crisis" up there in the state capitol.

It is useful to view the state legislature's celebration of thrift as a ceremonial function. The concept helps illuminate further the institutional preoccupation with old dogma, old doctrine, cherished but passé ideals.

At the same time, however, the concept requires the observer to think of this behavior as not quite rational. It does not seem altogether inappropriate to describe certain legislative behavior as irrational, but that is not to imply that it lacks meaning. In many aspects of their behavior human beings are irrational. Psychologists assure us, however, that the irrational appearance of behavior does not mean that it is without purpose. Behavior is purposeful though irrational. The purpose is to be detected in the effect of the behavior.

To ascertain the purpose of the state legislature's fiscal behavior it is necessary to recall the *true constituency* it serves. This is not the people. The legislature's true constituency (with the infrequent exception when a single strong leader becomes its true constituency) is composed of that loosely coalesced community of commercial interests enumerated previously, the corporate community of industry, finance and business—banking, realty, insurance, trucking, rails, liquor, mining (coal and minerals), fuels (oil and gas), sometimes gambling (horses, dogs, jai-alai), power (gas and electric utilities) and farming (when it takes on a corporate personality as in the Florida citrus industry).

It is this true constituency that the legislature protects with its celebrations of thrift. It protects the true constituency from carrying a reasonable share of the tax load. Anyone acquainted with the promotional literature published by the states to attract industry will be aware that they invariably boast of the light tax burden carried by business and commerce in the state. In addition, certain states offer specific tax forgiveness to incoming business. Truth is a rarity in some fields of promotion, but in this the states do not lie; an abundance of scholarly expert research exists as solid corroboration. It is a truism that the history of state taxation is a history of regressive direct personal consumer taxes combined with only slightly progressive income taxes; a persistent reluctance to tax business and industry has been part of that history. It will be useful to keep this commonplace in mind along the way to some deeper understanding of the legislative nature.

When the legislature creates the aura of fiscal crisis, it is to protect the true constituency, and this purpose usually becomes clear when the final act of the drama is played— when the legislature, after the appropriate celebration, agrees to a budget and tax program. If, of course, the budget is modest enough to be carried by existing taxes, then the true constituency has been protected only at the cost of procrastinating needed public improvements. If, on the other hand, the budget entails new taxes, the legislature ordinarily will assess them directly on the people, the theoretical constituency that the celebration of thrift neither serves nor protects.

A governor who senses this propensity of the legislature is frequently able to exploit it in setting the stage for new taxes. In such an instance, the legislature must simply be given a clear opportunity to dramatize its protective attitude toward the true constituency as it moves toward a new tax program. Often the legislature will create its own opportunity to dramatize its sympathies. Examples abound:

Virginia's general assembly for years followed the no-new-taxes course, achieving both low levies on the commercial community and wretched services for the people. "The condition of the state's mental hospitals," as the *Washington Post* pointed out March 9, 1966, ". . . has been very widely conceded for years to be a public scandal."

During these years, to be sure, the true constituency of the Virginia legislature was for the most part one leader, U.S. Senator Harry Byrd, whose own attitudes happened to coincide perfectly with those of the commercial community. In 1966 Byrd had just retired, and a new governor, Mills E. Godwin, Jr., took office. He asked the legislature to enact a sales tax and, according to form, sounded a crisis note:

"We can take no rest until all our public schools—not just some—will compare with any in the nation; until all our colleges and universities—not just some—can hold up their heads in any company; until all our sons and daughters—not just some—have the same chances to train their minds and their skills to the utmost. Nor can we rest there, for an educated people will demand, in fact already are demanding, that they be given the proper tools of our civilization with which to work." Godwin also reminded the legislature "of a continuing shortage of highway funds," adding the obvious: "The longer we wait to build them, the higher the cost of construction will be."

Privately, the state legislature seemed in a mood to enact the new sales tax at the outset. But a great furore followed first—along with collateral drama. This came in the form of a debate over the state's traditional pay-as-you-go policy which Byrd had first enforced in the 1920s. "We cannot count on our present revenues to finance commitments of the future," said Senator William B. Hopkins, leader of a group proposing to abandon the policy. To stick to pay-as-you-go means a "retreat from progress," he said. From the traditional side came the answer: to depart from pay-as-you-go would lead "to larger and larger deficits like the Federal Government."

Controversy raged on—although there was never the slightest chance that pay-as-you-go would be abandoned. The controversy ended with headlines billboarding the drama: "Virginia Senate Unit Kills Bill to Abolish Pay-as-You-Go Policy," said the *Washington Post*.

This done, tribute paid to the true constituency, the legislature got ready to enact the sales tax Godwin had asked for, starting at two per cent and escalating to three. One *Washington Post* reporter wrote from Richmond: "The last major action on the top priority sales tax measure came when the House, by a *surprising* two to one vote, reversed its earlier decision to knock Godwin's one per cent escalator clause out of the bill." It was not really so surprising. Generally, a state legislature goes along with a regressive tax once it has celebrated thrift and dramatized its sympathy for the true constituency.

In 1949 the governor of Florida was Fuller Warren, a flamboyant orator who was once described as "an indefatigable virtuoso of polysyllabic inconsequentialities." In fairness, the description caught the spirit of his rhetoric but not the genuine populist streak that was in him. At the outset of his administration Warren set the stage for a perfect illustration of the legislative behavior being discussed here.

Warren said the state was financially "strapped," and

could not finance needed public improvements on existing taxes. Then he proposed a series of taxes that, if enacted, would have hit almost every single segment of the legislature's true constituency. He asked for a severance tax on minerals and timber, he asked for a tax on banking and on private utilities—all the commercial entities then (and still) getting a nearly free ride.

The response in the legislature was Pavlovian. Wham, wham, wham, it killed every tax that the governor had proposed—then overwhelmingly "forced" a sales tax on him. There is sometimes more subtlety in the legislative behavior, and in the gubernatorial.

In Michigan, Governor Soapy Williams early in his administration (1949–61) began seeking a corporation profits tax to supplement the state's general sales tax. He got nowhere. Each time the proposal came up the lawmakers buried it; inevitably they complained that it would drive industry out of the state. Then in 1953, as it was recorded in James Reichley's *States in Crisis*, ". . . the legislature enacted a business activities tax, drawn up by lobbyists and economists for the automobile companies, which levied on the value added to products by business in Michigan." It was a complex law, and Williams let it take effect without his signature. The legislature, meanwhile, continued to give him regular increases in the taxes on liquor and cigarettes and petroleum, but still the state needed more money. The fiscal crisis seemed to have reached a historic climax in 1959. An adamant legislature let state employes go payless for five days beyond the scheduled pay time. It was a nationally publicized drama. And it was just at that time that Governor Williams was forced to accept more consumer taxes—until the state constitution could be amended to allow the legislature to raise the sales tax from three to four per cent.

It was not especially unusual, incidentally, for the Michigan legislature to enact a tax bill drafted by lobbyists. When the Arizona legislature recently increased the general sales tax by fifty per cent, according to *States in Crisis*, "credit for drafting the tax law was generally given to railroad lobbyist, A. M. (Bumps) Crawford, who died soon after. Ray Gilbert, lobbyist for the power utilities, also had a hand in drafting tax legislation during the session."

In Idaho, Governor Robert E. Smylie, proposing a New Day program in 1965 ("new days of achievement, of opportunity and self-reliance"), got swift approval of a new three per cent sales tax simply by making it part of a tax "reform" program—one that reduced income and property taxes by some $25 million. It allowed the legislature to increase expenditures for public schools by 42 per cent and still make an important tribute to the true constituency, with its special sensitivity to the income tax.

To mention a couple of more examples, in Massachusetts in 1966 Governor John Volpe sounded a most emphatic note of crisis as the legislature convened. "The need, so urgent and persistent, remains unmet. The dilemma, so chronic and critical, remains unsolved." The need he was talking about was money. But the dilemma, so chronic and critical, existed in the legislature. Six times in 1965 the governor had submitted a sales tax program to the legislature. Six times it was rejected. In 1966 he submitted it the seventh time, and finally, after eighteen months of elaborate controversy, it was enacted—after the legislature had been given the opportunity to turn down several other bills supported by sales tax opponents and providing major boosts in the income tax.

Massachusetts thus became the forty-first state to put a sales tax on the books. The legislature provided that it should be only temporary, to expire at the close of 1967. This is not an uncommon provision. West Virginia's three per cent sales tax was temporary for some time until the legislature last year made it permanent.

New Jersey in 1966 was one of but three states having no broad-based tax, neither on sales nor income. Heavily industrial, the state has jacked up property taxes steadily while its public programs have sagged sadly. Hughes issued the sound of crisis as the 1966 legislature convened.

"I am well aware," he said, "of the reluctance with which any legislator must approach a vote for a broad-based tax in a state which for a very long time has prided itself on the absence of such a tax. But that pride has been tarnished by our obvious shortcomings in the meeting of our public obligations. Therefore, I think that no legislator can expect reward for inaction that perpetuates such public neglect; indeed the exact opposite is more likely to follow."

With that, Hughes proposed an income tax as the "cornerstone of New Jersey's future." Not all legislators were impressed by his warning. "If it were a choice between the income tax and nothing," said Senator William E. Ozzard, "I would vote for nothing."

The governor's income tax program had hardly been revealed before numerous legislators were circulating a sales tax plan similar to Massachusetts' new one. By spring Hughes admitted: "I don't have enough votes to sustain any hope at the present time to enact a state income tax." Nevertheless, after long discussion of the fated income tax, the legislators a short time later handed Hughes a new sales tax law.

"If the voice of the people means anything," Hughes had told the convening legislature in a veiled reference to his landslide re-election in the fall of 1965, "it is a call to greatness, a call to achievement, a call to action."

Perhaps. But the state legislature is usually heeding a different voice.

14

". . . THE NOTION OF PARTY
RESPONSIBILITY FOR STATE
AFFAIRS OFTEN BECOMES
ALMOST COMPLETELY IRREL-
EVANT."

—Key,
American State Politics

★★★★★★★★★★★★★★★★★★★★
★★★★★★★★★★★★★★★★★★★★

One trait appears to be common to observers of human behavior: they are seldom content merely to observe human behavior.

They also wish to understand the mechanics of it. They hunger for explanations that are rational, lucid, ones that have the clear sting of reason—and yet provide emotional satisfaction.

This is not an ignoble desire. Indeed, this desire and its fulfillment may be the only alternative to despair and madness in a world of human beings.

The drawback is that while fulfillment is satisfying it almost inevitably blunts reason's sharp sting.

A man's reason alone, to illustrate, should assure him that the human race has ever been belligerent, murderous, destructive, cruel. Observations dictate this conclusion.

Yet, when a reasonable man observes an event in which the human race behaves belligerently, murderously, destructively, cruelly, he is not content with the fundamental knowledge that this is to be expected. He seeks emotionally satisfying explanations.

To the American, for example, this means identifying those barbaric traits with an alien ideology.

Hence, from the 1930s until 1945 Germans and Italians were murderous and destructive not because they were human but because they were Nazis and Fascists, as were the Japanese. Later the previously heroic Russians appeared to be barbaric because they were communists, and the Chinese visited murder, destruction and cruelty upon the world by proxy in Korea and Vietnam because they were communists, too.

Throughout this period, obviously, the human race has behaved just as it always has. Only the explanations have changed.

Such explanations are not only respectable but highly satisfying emotionally. The need for them is attested by the fact that society produces legions of writers, pundits, commentators, philosophers, politicians, statesmen and diplomats to show how all these unfortunate events are caused by alien creeds.

Among the Turks of the Middle Ages it is not difficult to imagine a pundit called Omar Alsop who provided equivalent satisfaction by explaining with comparable logic why those minions of Peter the Hermit and Walter the Penniless had tramped across a continent to let the blood of people they had never seen before. To the pundits of the East the Crusades no doubt appeared to represent a relentless strategy of world conquest by the Christians, and this explanation doubtless helped assuage the anxieties of the common folk who wondered why the hell everybody was fighting all the time.

The unsatisfactory thing about this kind of explanation is that it tends to make the man of reason forget the essential truth that he knew all along: that the human race has ever been belligerent, murderous, destructive and cruel and is capable of inventing ten thousand reasons to justify it.

That gratuitous soliloquy was but a prelude to a reminder that the observer should not be distracted too severely by the conventional explanations that are advanced to account for the behavior of the state legislature.

One habitual—and shrugging—way of accounting for it lies in the they-are-only-human diagnosis. One hears hundreds of legislators convert this to a we-are-only-human rationalization, yet there are serious journalists who also resort to it. "The public often is critical of the legislature and the laws it produces," wrote the *Courier-Journal's* pundit Hugh Morris. "Much of the criticism is rooted in a failure to realize that these are not supermen, but ordinary citizens with limited skills, seeking the synthesis of ideas, desires and understandings that is the very heart of the democratic process."

One must seriously wonder where on earth this pundit ever encountered anyone who regarded state legislators as supermen. But beyond that, one must remember that the human frailty of individual members does not account for the *institutional* behavior. Members of the Mafia are only human, but it is the nature of their institution that accounts for much of their behavior. Or, to employ a more optimistic illustration, members of the Catholic priesthood are only human, but it is obviously not their humanity that leads them to celibacy. It is the institution.

Easily the most prevalent of our habitual and conventional ways of interpreting legislative behavior is in terms of partisan politics. The activity that I categorize as the celebration of thrift (the initial resistance to a budget, the initial resistance to taxation, the insistence on tribute to the true constituency) is commonly portrayed as the result of partisan struggle, a contest of some kind between Democrats and Republicans.

In Massachusetts, for example, where the legislature first resisted then enacted new taxes, political journalists sought to explain the behavior in terms of the fact that Democrats controlled the legislature while a Republican occupied the governor's chair. It was true, of course, that Democrats controlled the legislature while it was refusing to enact taxes, but it is equally true that they still controlled when the legislature did enact taxes.

It is further true that the Massachusetts legislature's initial behavior toward a sales tax program did not differ substantially in 1956, when Democrat Foster Furcolo was governor and the Democrats controlled the House and the

Republicans the Senate. Nor in 1958, when, as *States in Crisis* put it, "Furcolo was even less successful with the new legislature, completely controlled by Democrats, than he had been with the last, in which the Republicans held the Senate. Not only was the sales tax again defeated by an overwhelming majority in the House, but . . ." various other salient features of the gubernatorial program went down the drain. In the light of these past events, party appears to be incidental to the legislature's behavior in Massachusetts, where it does not differ substantially from that of any other legislature.

In New York as in other states an aura of fiscal crisis has emanated from the state capitol. When Nelson Rockefeller took office as governor he touched off the usual kind of controversy by asking the Republican-run legislature to enact a new tax law that the opposition accurately dubbed a "rich man's relief bill." It provided that kind of "reform" in the income tax—lifting the rates in the lower brackets and moderating them in the upper and corporate brackets. After a suitable amount of celebration the Republican-run legislature passed it.

In 1964, however, the New York assembly fell into Democratic control for the first time in a generation. Republican Rockefeller was still governor, though, and the aura of fiscal crisis naturally recurred in 1965. The Republican governor asked the Democratic legislature to enact a sales tax, and after a suitable period of controversy it passed one. The New York press, having followed its conventional practice of assuming that a Democratic legislature would necessarily be in deep conflict with a Republican governor, accounted for the enactment of the sales tax by assuming further that it resulted from some mysterious "deal" between the Republican Rockefeller and the then Democratic mayor of New York City, Robert Wagner.

Actually, the 1965 legislature was simply behaving characteristically, as does any state legislature except under extraordinary circumstances. Both the usually Democratic legislature of Massachusetts and the usually Republican legislature of New York reduced the tax load carried by corporations by about one-half between 1948 and 1961, and by 1966 both states had a sales tax on the books. In all of the prosperous 1950s not a single state added a new income tax to the books.

One of the classic contemporary instances of a fiscal "impasse" between a governor and a legislature is the occasion, already mentioned, when the Michigan legislature allowed state employes to go without their pay for a few days while the legislature refused to enact Governor Soapy Williams' tax laws. To reiterate, the legislature finally compelled Williams to accept more direct consumer taxes rather than enact equitable taxes on the commercial community. I have read a score or so of analyses of this situation, and with little variation commentators place great weight upon the fact that Soapy Williams was a Democrat and the legislature dominated by Republicans. In short, the conventional interpretation was drawn with various shadings.

From this distance, however, it is plain that the only unusual thing about the legislature's behavior was its dramatic excess. In allowing the state payday to pass by it was simply indulging in unusual irresponsibility to dramatize its position with unusual emphasis. Otherwise, this behavior was characteristic, a truth that would be easier to perceive if our span of attention were longer.

The behavior of the Michigan legislature has not differed substantially under Republican Governor George Romney. It was Republican-run when he first took office and subsequently, because of reapportionment and the 1964 Democratic landslide, fell into the hands of the other party. Every clipping I have read indicates that an aura of fiscal crisis has continued to hang over the capitol—even in 1966 when the state found itself with a substantial surplus of money, as well as in 1965 when the legislature, after suitable controversy, appropriated some $32 million more than the governor had asked for.

Recently the national press began taking note of how the butt-headed Democratic legislature at Olympia, Washington, was delivering such a trouncing to an appealing young Republican governor named Daniel Evans. He had overcome tremendous Democratic odds to emerge as a bright star of the GOP, and the substance of the story was that it was something fierce to see the Democratic legislature take him to pieces. The only trouble with the story was that it was written while the legislature was in the middle of its celebration of thrift as well as other diversions, including a reapportionment dispute. By the end of the session the Democratic legislature decided to hand the Republican governor $59 million in additional taxes, consumer taxes naturally. It raised the sales tax from 4 to 4.2 per cent and the cigarette tax from seven to eleven cents a pack, not forgetting boosts in the rates on other tobacco products and liquor.

Apart from the evidence that has presented itself perennially in the South (where solidly Democratic legislatures under uniformly Democratic governors exhibit behavior exactly like that found in the North), other events in other capitols so frequently discredit the partisan interpretation of legislative actions that one wonders how the convention survives. One supposes there has been a general surrender to that convenient temptation to assume that a legislature should behave according to the predilections of its individual members. Usually, it does not. The individual members generally behave in accordance with the institutional predilections of the legislature. And its true constituency does not vote a party line.

The state legislature's sympathetic relationship with its true constituency is not a mirage.

It can be detected in existing state law.

It is reflected in the legislature's fiscal policies.

It shows itself in the legislature's preoccupations during a session.

It is often blatantly apparent in the composition of committees.

It can be heard in legislative rhetoric. Even the very

habitual reference to government as a "business" reveals the intimacy of the legislature's identification with the true constituency. Government obviously is not engaged in the pursuit of profit. It is not a business.

Finally, the state legislature's relationship to its true constituency begins to reveal itself most profoundly as one begins to perceive the degree of the legislature's alienation from its theoretical constituency, the people.

It is this alienation that has made the partisan composition of the legislature almost totally irrelevant to its behavior.

Thus it is not merely idle iconoclasm to discredit the conventional mode of interpreting legislative actions. It is an essential step in the process of discovering what really is happening.

In itself, the alienation of the state legislature from the people is hardly news. There is an obvious, manifest and widespread impression that it is remote from the mainstream of American life. This impression finds voice in a variety of words.

"State government," wrote Dick McDonald, executive secretary of the National Conference of State Legislative Leaders, "it is frequently said these days [1965], is the *forgotten* battleground of the American federal system."

Similar language came to the mind of Mrs. Robert J. Stuart, national president of the League of Women Voters. "State government," she said also in 1965, "has sometimes been called 'the forgotten branch.' It has been neglected too long, but . . ." The League was promoting a "Focus on State Government" program.

At a meeting of the National Legislative Conference in Portland, Oregon, Field Director George Morgan of the Citizens' Conference on State Legislation told what must be done to improve legislation. "The first thing," he said, "must be that legislators themselves are willing to have their institution looked at closely. The second thing is that people from all walks of life must become interested and develop an understanding of their legislatures."

Plainly, the condition of the legislature's remoteness is widely perceived. The causes of it are not as widely understood. From almost all sources one hears wistful variations of George Morgan's proposal. *People must become interested.* This could be documented ad infinitum because it is a standard political sermon familiar to all.

The implication is that the legislature is as it is because the people are disinterested. The observer who probes further will discover that the reverse is true. In becoming what they are, legislatures have historically and steadily and increasingly isolated themselves from the people.

Some ways in which this was accomplished were the subject of one of Key's books, *American State Politics.* His purpose was not to condemn the legislature but to plumb the relationships between political parties and state government.

What his study revealed, however, was that state legislatures have managed to write election laws that effectively minimize the weight of parties in state government and all but deny the people access to the government through the ballot. It is not the apportionment problem Key was talking about when he wrote: "The institutions and electoral procedures . . . have been more or less deliberately designed to frustrate popular majorities."

In establishing that parties are of little consequence in state government Key more or less followed the political science tradition of elaborately documenting what common sense and close observation suggests is true. Still, in doing this he showed more vividly than anyone else that this has been the result of both conscious and unconscious legislative policy. He further demonstrated how, as state government has become more insulated from the popular will, the interest of the people has plummeted. Unless there is a big federal election to bring them out the people hardly bother to vote in state contests. Key sampled the election returns of fifteen nonsouthern states over a long period, from 1926 to 1952. "In three out of four primaries not more than 35 per cent of the potential electorate voted in the primaries of one or the other of the major parties," he reported. At best, more than 50 per cent of the potential vote turned out in only one of twelve primaries. The usual portion of the potential electorate voting: 25 to 35 per cent.

Key succinctly stated the nature of the cycle that operates continually as a consequence of policies designed to minimize the influence and power of the voter. Low interest results first. Then: "The low priority of voter concern about state affairs affects the problems of political leadership . . . The character of the leadership may also in turn contribute to the low level of public interest."

Partly by encouraging this cycle has the state legislature become "forgotten," remote, alienated and too often irrelevant and unresponsive to all elements except the true constituency.

In the conventional lore, the state legislature is said to go through its regular rituals over taxes and expenditures out of concern for what the voters may think. The implication is that what the voters think and do has great bearing on the legislature's behavior. Especially in the competition of two-party politics, according to this lore, the issues will have been refined and the voters will make a choice and their wishes will be carried out in the legislature.

It is not easy to measure the validity of this part of the conventional lore. But it has been measured—at least the effect of party competition on policy. A political scientist from the University of Georgia, Thomas R. Dye, conducted a study under the elaborate controls for which his profession is famed. He selected twenty-eight policy issues, all subject to perennial legislative activity. The issues included such as "public school expenditures per pupil in average daily attendance 1960–61," and "public school expenditures per capita" and "per capita state expenditures for higher education." The study also covered spending for welfare, unemployment compensation, aid to dependent children.

When it was done Dye delivered the paper at the 1965 meeting of the American Political Science Association. The auditorium in Washington's Sheraton-Park hotel rang with phrases like "socio-economic inputs" and "political system variables" and "feedback linkage" and "conceptual framework" as Professor Dye worked his politically scientific way toward a conclusion. His conclusion was:

"In short, party competition has *no apparent independent effect* [his emphasis] on twenty-six of the twenty-eight policy outcomes investigated."

There may well be parties to be blamed for the behavior of the state legislature, but evidently they are not the Democratic or the Republican.

15

★★★★★★★★★★★★★★★★★★★★★
★★★★★★★★★★★★★★★★★★★★★

"WHERE THE CARCASE IS
THERE WILL THE VULTURES
BE GATHERED TOGETHER."
—Bryce

★★★★★★★★★★★★★★★★★★★★★
★★★★★★★★★★★★★★★★★★★★★

To perceive the state legislature's alienation from the people is but a step toward perceiving the intricate and pervasive intimacy of the legislature's relationship with its true constituency.

It is this relationship that accounts for most of the legislature's salient idiomorphic characteristics, those that have been the subject of perennial discussion and perpetual dismay since the founding of the Republic.

It is a relationship, moreover, that has never been adequately treated in the conventional lore.

In fact, the commonly used concepts and phrases of the conventional lore tend to veil the nature and depth of the relationship. It is common journalistic practice, for example, to speak of the various segments of the commercial community as "special interests." These "special interests" send representatives called "lobbyists" to the state legislature. Through these "lobbyists" the "special interests" exercise the right of petition. Hence the "lobbyists" attempt to persuade the legislature to enact laws that benefit the "special interests." When the "lobbyists" provide the legislature with certain material benefits that exceed some uncertain limit "corruption" is the result. A legislator who has some highly particular and formalized standing with a "special interest" is said to be susceptible to a "conflict of interest."

Such, simplified, are the conventional journalistic and academic concepts. They mislead in several ways, the primary and general one being that it simply does not happen quite that way. The notion of "special interests" suggests in the first place a separateness and distance that do not exist between the commercial community and the legislature. Similarly misleading is the notion that the "special interests" send "lobbyists" all the way to the capitol to persuade.

Actually, the relationship between the commercial community and the legislature is so close that their identities often tend to meld. And after attentive study the observer will begin to see that the "lobbyists" for the "special interests," while they may infrequently function as persuaders (mostly when one "special interest" falls in conflict with another "special interest"), they play a more general institutional role.

Collectively, the "special interests" are the true constituency of the legislature, and collectively the "lobbyists" appear as delegates from the true constituency, a corporate liaison, a working directorate that in most cases simply conveys the will of the commercial community and coordinates the implementation of its wishes by the legislature.

The conventional lore misleads in suggesting that these "lobbyists" come to the legislature as mere supplicants. As a rule they do not. They come as the emissaries and minions of prevalent power. (Lobbyists for the theoretical constituency, the people, do come as supplicants, however. In the conventional lore there has been a persistent and seemingly studious effort to confuse lobbyists for the public, say, those for public education, with those who represent the true constituency. "After all," this line goes, "these are special interests, too." Such willful confusion may be attributable to the close identification of the advertising-supported press with the interests of the commercial community.) Finally, the conventional lore misleads in the basic premise upon which it rests its usual concepts—the assumption of an independent-minded legislature to which "special interests" must send "lobbyists" to obtain sympathetic consideration.

The actuality, evident in the entire history of the subject, is that the state legislature has never existed as an independent-minded institution. In its earliest origins and throughout its history it has functioned as an instrumentality of the commercial community.

It is this long-lasting intimacy that the conventional lore tends to befog. The observer should undertake no purely semantic quarrel with the use of the term "special interest." It has been and will remain a useful part of the vocabulary of state politics. Yet, it does not suggest the way the legislature's mentality has been intertwined with and subordinate to that of the commercial community over the years. It is to convey an idea of this relationship more emphatically that I have chosen to use the term *true constituency*.

In this relationship the observer will at length perceive the reasons for legislative behavior that has preoccupied and puzzled political observers for generations. This relationship by and large accounts for every legislative characteristic that has dismayed the people, deepened the alienation of the legislature and reduced its relevancy to the development of the American society.

One of the ironies of this actuality is that the state legislature's relationship with the commercial community has retained its historic cast even while the commercial community itself, in its most substantial components, has radically altered its own role in American society; it has thus retained its relevancy in the role that the new conventional wisdom holds to be that of one countervailing force in the great triumvirate of countervailing forces: big business, big labor, big government.

In this scheme, state government dribbles along in its eddies of obsolescence. It is at least interesting to speculate that the substantial corporate community retains the legislature in the old relationship of subordination only as a way of celebrating the good old days when business pushed all government around. This speculation is commended by several considerations: certainly the goodies that the commercial community elicits from the state legislature are trivial in the total picture of today's corporate world; yet today's corporate world quite likely obtains great and satisfying psychic income simply by dominating *some* government as it did in the days of free-booting capitalism. Certainly the day has long passed when it can dominate the federal government (as several recent presidents have indicated to the steel industry, among others). So it may just be at least partly for emotional rewards that the commercial community continues the affair at the state capitol, an affair so reminiscent of the day when it had the upper hand all over. After all, the commercial world too clings emotionally to the past. It too is forever talking about the American free-enterprise system, as though it existed still.

Whatever, the relationship accounts for several pronounced elements of legislative character and behavior that will be the subjects of the concluding sections of these comments. Because of this relationship the legislature appears ethically obtuse and corruption-ridden; because of it the legislature has experienced those crippling and chronic anxieties about a mostly imaginary loss of power; because of it the legislature became a nearly volitionless serf to an antidemocratic syndrome that, while accounting for its systematic foreclosure of the popular will, as Key perceived, also accounts for its historic dereliction on reapportionment.

Because of this relationship, moreover, there is scarcely a chance that even widespread and fair reapportionment will noticeably increase the relevancy of the state in the continuing development of the society. It is to this lack of relevancy that so many refer, consciously or not, when they speak of state government as the forgotten branch. It is to this lack of relevancy that I refer when I speak of the fall of the states.

When Americans do remember the "forgotten branch" they tend to think of it as habitually corrupt. One reason for this is that the typical citizen seldom thinks about his state legislature at all except during those periodic public scandals that have so much human interest about them.

At such moments the usually remote legislature becomes a timely reality, and the citizen pays close attention to the news reports about it. Thus it seems to many that every time they read about the legislature it is reeking of scandal.

Corruption, in turn, comes to be associated with the feelings of futility that people experience when regarding the state legislature. Actually, fresh news of corruption only reminds the people of feelings of futility that were already there.

Nevertheless, one result of the sporadic scandal is to make many observers think that the legislature performs as it does *because* it is corrupt. In this view corruption is construed as a cause of the legislative tendency to give the interests of its true constituency preference over the public interest.

In the long measure, however, the observer may find it illuminating to consider corruption as an *effect* rather than a cause of the legislature's relationship with the true constituency.

This is not to split hairs: obviously, specific legislative derelictions have been reasonably attributed to specific instances of bribery. Cold cash has caused votes to be cast in a certain way. Yet the general ethical climate in which this occurs may be fairly viewed as an effect of, an outgrowth of the legislature's relationship with the true constituency.

"Corruption," as one investigator summed up after a grand jury investigation of skullduggery in California back in 1938, "is not necessarily bribery. The term is a general one suggesting loss of integrity—a taint. Instances of bribery encountered in the investigation were relatively few . . . The principal source of corruption has been 'money pressure.' "

Except where specified this broad meaning of the word is intended here.

In this sense of the word, then, corruption has flowed inevitably from the role that the legislature has played in American society. In its origins the legislature was purely an organ of commerce, and the customs and traditions of mind formed in the period of nativity have never disappeared. Originally, of course, there was no call for a legislature to distinguish between the business of the people and the business of business. The state legislature was an organ of business pure and simple. The Massachusetts legislature, for example, was only the board of directors (General Court) of a profit-making corporation. Later it evolved ostensibly into the people's instrumentality. But it would have been surprising had it suddenly chosen to draw a distinction between its duty to commerce and its duty to the people. The force of custom is an awesome thing in human institutions.

Further, on top of this intimacy, the sheer longevity of the relationship between the commercial community and the legislature is such that continued commercial intercourse between them may be regarded as inevitable. In a sense the legislature and its true constituency are like kissing cousins who have let their affection get out of hand.

Both the antiquity and intimacy of the relationship makes it seem the most natural and respectable thing in the world to most lawmakers themselves. A state legislator often seems simply confounded or perplexed when someone —a fellow member or an outsider even—raises questions about "conflicts of interest."

Every newspaper reader is familiar with the line that a lawmaker takes when he is criticized, for instance, for accepting fees from a private enterprise that has an interest in legislation. The lawmaker will express astonishment that anyone might question his conduct. Often his remarks will have noticeable overtones of piety.

As one example, consider the words of Paul Powell, the Illinois secretary of state who was accused of receiving cash fees and cheap stock from race-track interests that he had helped while still an influential legislator. Powell, who pushed legislation that gave the tracks longer seasons and lower taxes, had no qualms at all about being offered the low-priced stock. "My only mistake was that I didn't get more," he said. And as for receiving a "finder's fee" of $8,000 a year from Irwin S. (Big Sam) Wiedrick, an ex-convict closely tied to Illinois racing, Powell explained that it was for dealings in real estate, adding: "My dealings with Wiedrick are completely legal, legitimate, honest and honorable, unless making money has now been declared to be a crime. This income has kept me free from bribes or acting in any way in conflict of office."

Or, as another example, consider a concept of public service advanced by former New York State Senator Mac-Neil Mitchell, co-sponsor of the Mitchell-Lama Housing Law of 1955. In 1966 Mitchell was testifying before a state investigation committee about some $427,000 that his law firm received as fees for organizing state-financed housing projects while Mitchell was head of a joint legislative committee on housing. Mitchell saw nothing even questionable about his having helped organize the projects that produced the fees while holding that legislative position. "Far from having any conflict of interest," he said, "we were performing a public service."

The observer may find it useful to ponder these responses. Often the accused lawmaker is entirely sincere. He actually does not see anything wrong. Lectures about "conflict" of interest make no sense to him simply because between the lawmaker and his true constituency there is complete mutuality of interest. In short there *is* no conflict. One may encounter this attitude among men of sterling personal honesty and considerable sensitivity.

One of the touching stories I heard in state politics involved an honest and sensitive politician named LeRoy Collins, Florida's governor from 1955 through 1960. Collins is a generally high-minded individual who established a national reputation later as president of the National Association of Broadcasters, then as head of the Federal Community Relations Service, the new race relations branch of the national Administration.

In Tallahassee, where he lived, Collins served for some fourteen years in the state senate and won high praise from reporters who observed his legislative performance. In private life he was a well-to-do lawyer who represented big corporate clients including a railroad whose cases he argued from time to time before the State Railroad and Public Utilities Commission. When Collins sought the governorship an opponent criticized him for practicing law before the state commission while serving in the state senate. The criticism dismayed Collins. To a friend he asked: "Is he saying that I have been doing something *wrong*?" The teller of this story recalled that, at length, someone reflected that under federal law a congressman engaging in comparable practice before a government commission would be subject to a sentence of several years in prison and a fine of several thousand dollars. There was no Florida state law prohibiting this kind of thing, which, of course, was commonplace.

Where there is no law legislators often are not merely feigning naïveté when they profess to perceive no conflict. The practice of a legislator serving in a dual role has in most places the approval of long custom. However, one can hardly imagine a judge who is receiving fees from an insurance company failing to disqualify himself from a case in which the company appears as a party; the temptation to presume bias if he presided would be overwhelming.

This rudimentary ethical question has long since been settled within the institution of the law. On the other hand it is commonplace for the legislator-lawyer to receive fees from a company that he must deal with in writing regulatory and tax laws. The presumption of bias is just as strong in this instance, but the ethical question has been generally and historically excluded from the arena of the state legislature.

As a usual thing, in fact, the state legislature tends to follow a policy quite the opposite of that prevailing in the judiciary; that is, if a legislator is directly and financially interested in some segment of the commercial community the common practice is to allow him extraordinary privileges in that field of legislation. His expertise is well regarded.

Thus one frequently finds full-time bankers or directors of banks holding influential posts on banking committees.

Insurance men regularly participate in writing the codes that regulate the insurance industry. Every observer is probably familiar with such examples; they break into print regularly. These are cases where a conflict of interest is obvious and intrinsic.

This kind of practice, however, is merely an outgrowth of the intimate relationship that exists between the legislature and its true constituency. Where a banker determines the content of the banking laws the legislative identity, of course, melds totally into that of the true constituency. In the mind of such a banker-legislator there is no conflict of interest because there is no conflict of identity. When criticized or challenged, the banker-legislator is likely to insist that he *will* serve the public interest in considering the legislation that comes before him. A judge in a comparable position would be hooted out of court by the bar association and conceivably impeached by the legislature.

The ethical world of the legislature can be most clearly perceived from the outside. But the observer, if he wishes to plumb the legislative mind, must remember that a situation which to him appears to involve conflict does not, to the typical lawmaker, involve any such thing. The legislative behavior is shaped by a set of institutional standards that spring from its relationship with the true constituency, so— except in special instances—if the legislature has merely served that constituency it simply does not comprehend the critic who says that it has behaved in an unethical way.

This state of mind has become as natural to the legislator as the attitude of the lawyer who defends a known racketeer; the criminal lawyer would consider himself unethical only if he failed to provide the best defense possible. This comparison is not intended in any way to equate the philosophies that have been constructed to justify the latter attitude or the former; it is intended to suggest that one state of mind is as deeply rooted as the other, even though each is rooted in a different concept of what constitutes the public interest.

As a rule a legislature becomes upset not when its code of conduct conflicts with the public interest, which is regularly, but when its code is dramatized in such a way that the public becomes sharply aware of the conflict and responds with a brief show of outrage. Further, at these moments the legislature is not upset because of the breach of ethics, which it seldom even perceives, but at the failure of the public to "understand" its behavior.

As an illustration, one might take the case of a florid, affable, gray-haired man named Raeburn C. Horne, now dead, who was a former Florida state senator who subsequently for many years represented important segments of the small-loan industry in its relations with the legislature. It was well reported and common knowledge that the small-loan industry always got what it wished out of the Florida legislature. As well, it was common knowledge that Horne had the closest possible relationship with the lawmakers personally and collectively. He entertained them habitually and well. Often when the ruling bloc of the senate—a coalition known as the Pork Chop Gang—had a "secret" strategy conference the secret would be published in all the papers along with the intelligence that the meeting was being held at a remote fishing camp, one operated by Horne, the small-loan representative. In short, there were no questions left about Horne's intimacy with the legislature. He was from Madison, Florida, and a very close friend of State Senator W. Turner Davis of Madison, once president of the senate and for years the perennial chairman of the powerful senate rules committee. Nobody was ever surprised that Horne's will seemed to prevail in the senate. He never did badly in the house either.

Nevertheless, one session in the late 1950s, when the Florida legislature was about to enact another bill benefiting the small-loan industry (one proposed, naturally, as a "reform" bill), a house member saw that Horne was sitting in the gallery casually wig-wagging parliamentary signals to the bill's floor manager. Note of this fact was taken on the floor of the house, and there was a flurry of publicity and public indignation. The legislature was momentarily upset.

Yet, nobody, no attentive observer, had learned anything new about legislative behavior; it had only been effectively dramatized. Momentarily the house appeared in the role of stooges to a puppeteer sitting in the gallery. This mandated an expression of outrage by the press and the public. The legislature generally, however, was not critical of its relationship with the small-loan industry but only of this dramatization of it. Subsequent conversations about the episode did not revolve around ethical questions but about questions of public relations. The legislature's momentary pique was expressed by the senator who said, "I don't see what everybody's excited about." Its enduring attitude was dramatized by the fact that it passed the bill. It doubled to $600 the maximum amount that a small-loan operator could legally lend.

As a postscript, when Horne died, State Senator W. Turner Davis, having been defeated in a race for re-election, succeeded him as a small-loan industry representative. This occasioned no excited comment except briefly when the senate in one session publicly called on the former rules chairman to interpret a parliamentary question. Subsequently, some senators proved sufficiently sensitive to realize that the practice of soliciting parliamentary guidance from a small-loans representative in just this way might create an unfavorable public impression. Again, this episode only dramatized a relationship that had long existed; it neither changed nor expanded it.

The small-loan industry had obtained an enduring place in the Florida legislature's true constituency, as the industry has in most states. The intimacy of the relationship revealed itself in action and oratory. Small-loan bills ("loan-shark" bills, the crusading press called them) could be counted on to prompt speeches in which respectable banker-legislators would praise the humanitarianism of an industry willing to lend money at thirty-six per cent interest a year to little people too risky for conventional lending institutions to bank on. Just so, the "public interest" was said to be served by legislation that enabled small-loan companies to save banks the stress of taking these unusual risks.

In the course of such debates an observer could perceive that it was quite impossible for the legislature to avoid identifying the public interest with the interests of the small loan companies and the banks. These were the constituents actually being served.

Moreover, any legislator who could distinguish the public interest and rose to defend it was invariably one of those few mavericks who operate outside of the main currents of legislative events. Dissent on ethical grounds is "maverick" behavior and recognized as such in every legislature only because it is so profoundly uncharacteristic.

In 1964 State Senator Paul Simon of Illinois won for himself an enduring reputation as a maverick. He wrote an article entitled "The Illinois Legislature—A Study in Corruption." *Harper's* published it in the September 1964 issue. Simon set it up by quoting from the U.S. Supreme Court's reapportionment opinion. "State legislators," the court had said, "are, historically, the fountainhead of representative government in this country." Simon added: ". . . There is little doubt that these fountainheads of democracy are . . . polluted almost beyond belief." Simon, a newspaperman by trade, drew on ten years' experience as a legislator to make points about several aspects of legislative behavior:

1. He estimated that about a third of the legislators take payoffs—some in the form of payments for legal services, public relations work or as campaign contributions, some fewer in the shape of undisguised bribes.

2. He sketched a technique of inviting payoffs. It involved the use of what in Illinois is called a "fetcher" bill—a measure that, by threatening to curtail some commercial interest, provides incentive for a payoff to obtain the death of the bill.

3. He documented the subservience of the legislature to the racing interests on both taxation and regulatory matters.

4. He noted the absence of controls on lobbyists and of safeguards between "the public's and the legislators' private interests."

5. He recorded how one senator, the owner of a finance

company, attended the wishes of the small-loan industry, how another represented the highway construction industry.

6. He explained how legislative budgets are fashioned "by a self-perpetuating clique behind closed doors."

7. He recalled how, during a "financial crisis" of the 1950s, the legislature increased the sales tax by 50 per cent —while passing another bill that reduced by a third the taxes on two prosperous race tracks.

8. He also noted that when he and a colleague publicly protested the bill reducing the racing taxes, requesting the governor to veto it, the legislative leaders responded by proposing a formal censure of the two as "men who lacked integrity" and had "disgraced" the legislature.

All these matters Paul Simon discussed under the subject of "corruption," his intention being to dissent from his legislature's practices. For so doing he was widely criticized by the legislature. Once he was nominated for a "Benedict Arnold Award," a suggestion the lawmakers amiably applauded during one formal senate dinner.

On the surface the lawmakers seemed to be scorning Paul Simon for betraying the legislature itself. But some reflection suggests that his actual offense was in betraying the true constituency. Only because the legislature's traditional loyalties lie elsewhere did Simon's stand with the public interest suggest the notion of treason.

Similarly, when the legislature accused Simon of a lack of "integrity," it accurately reflected the qualities that attach to the word in a state legislature. The legislature experiences a loss of integrity, its wholeness, when there is a breach with the true constituency. So intimate is the relationship that the legislature feels an incompleteness when the breach occurs. Hence the person causing or threatening to cause a breach appears to be causing or threatening a loss of integrity. So much a long communion tends.

By now the observer may have realized that all Simon actually recorded in his article were examples of behavior that is characteristic of the state legislature wherever it sits.

What Simon did not perceive, or did not write in any event, is how this behavior invariably springs from the legislature's relationship with its true constituency.

On the contrary, one import of Simon's article, as his opening paragraph showed, is that these characteristics might be changed by the proper and fair apportionment of the Illinois legislature. "The reforms that will follow are long overdue," he said. It is a point to be examined later.

It ought to be observed here, however, that from time immemorial the locus of the true constituency's power has been in the cities, and they have nonetheless commanded the service of the rural-dominated legislature. It would seem folly to assume that the true constituency will command less control if more legislators are to be selected from areas in which its power is most concentrated.

Simon himself, in telling how he discovered what a "fetcher bill" was, recounted how he hoped to sponsor legislation that might trim the absurdly high interest rates that public districts and municipalities were paying. He thus sponsored a measure to require competitive bidding on public bond issues.

Then a colleague in the house, where Simon then served, demanded: "What are you doing with my bill?"

"What bill?"

"That bond bill. I always introduce it, and I do rather well with it."

Simon turned down the invitation to suppress the bill himself. Subsequently, he recorded, the measure was sent to a committee "whose members had never before shown any interest in this subject." The committee got Simon to set a hearing, a prerogative of a bill's sponsor. He did and various groups came forward to endorse the bill. There was the Taxpayers Federation and the Farm Bureau among other groups in favor. Simon concluded: "There was virtually no opposition. Whereupon the eager committee killed the bill by a vote of twenty to nothing, and I could only wonder why."

The reason was hardly the mathematically unrepresentative nature of the Illinois legislature. The people who got shafted by that committee lived all over the state. The financial industry, ever a segment of the true constituency, cannot be defined in terms of a geographic area, though most of its main offices are in the cities. It nonetheless got effective representation in this instance.

In such a case one need not, in seeking some conclusion about the legislative character, assume that bribery was involved. In fact, had it occurred, bribery would have been mere passing, ancillary corruption. The prior and persisting corruption is a quality implicit in the relationship between the legislature and the financial industry, an ancient and enduring consortium. It is, in a way, a corruption of identity.

Ostensibly a *public* instrumentality, the legislature historically has actually functioned as an adjunct of its true constituency and thus exists under more or less fraudulent credentials. Even if not so much as a scotch and water passed hands between the financial industry and the committee that killed Simon's bill, the action may be viewed nonetheless as the product of corruption and not in the least surprising.

In the conventional lore the deeper institutional character of the state legislature is usually overlooked in the cataloguing of particular evils. Our habit of thought is to identify corruption only with its visible techniques. In scores of books and pamphlets that I have read about the state legislature (and, I confess, in many of the millions of words I wrote on the subject as a newspaper reporter), this habit of thought is nearly constant. A visible evil is identified, and then the analysis abruptly terminates after a peroration in which it is urged that the legislature ought to put a stop to it. A long list of "evils" have been recorded. At this point consider the "fetcher bill" evil which Illinois Senator Paul Simon discovered in Springfield.

The fetcher bill is a common phenomenon to the state legislature. At various times and places it has been called a "blackmail bill," a "shakedown bill," a "jingle bill," a "blackbag bill," a "satchel grabber" and a "Mae West bill," the latter designation invented to evoke Mae's classic invitation: "Come up and see me sometime."

The fetcher bill, briefly, is a technique that some legislators employ to induce certain segments of the commercial community to give them money or other benefits. The technique can be directed at almost any segment of the true constituency. Obviously, not every bill aimed at banking or trucking or liquor or racing or timber or utilities or chain stores is a fetcher bill. Yet any of these industries, among others, can be the target.

For this reason, the fetcher bill evil cannot be discussed meaningfully as though it resulted from mere individual corruption. The truth is that when a fetcher bill is introduced almost every member of the legislature realizes it at once. An observer familiar with the scene can often detect this first by the grins that flash around the chamber and later by the acknowledgments made in common conversation. The sponsor of a fetcher bill may not be a highly respected legislator, but he is invariably one whose behavior is dependably in accord with the prevailing legislative currents. He commonly supports the majority in its dealings with the commercial community. Almost by definition he is never a maverick, inasmuch as a maverick is a legislator who might sponsor a comparable bill with every intention of trying to get it passed. A distinctly different mood prevails in the legislature when a maverick introduces a bill that would hurt the true constituency. A certain cynical levity attends the processing of a fetcher.

When a fetcher bill is introduced there is a general appreciation of its true intentions. Otherwise, this technique of raising money would never work. Nor would it work if there were not an intimate relationship between the true constituency and the legislature. A victimized industry responds appropriately in this situation only because it assumes that the sponsor of a fetcher bill is approachable and the preponderance of the membership acquiescent and sympathetic. Any transaction that ensues between a victimized industry and legislators can hardly seem extraordinary in a milieu in which commercial intercourse is commonplace between them. Moreover, members of the legislature who might feel moral compunctions about this are seldom required to take a stand at all. With hardly an exception the fetcher bill is disposed of by a stacked committee—one that probably would not in any event have approved legislation that might curtail the victim industry.

This situation alone imparts to any "bribe" the nature of a normal tribute, or gratuity. That is, a fetcher-bill sponsor usually delivers no service that would not have been delivered anyway. All he does is provide an opportunity by introducing the bill. Mavericks who might dissent to all this on ethical grounds never have the opportunity. They will not be found in positions of importance on committees. They will have few occasions to dissent on the floor because fetcher bills do not often get that far.

The fetcher-bill technique, of course, need not be employed directly against an industry that is to be tapped. For example, a bill that would improve the competitive position of the trucking industry can be counted on to arouse the interest of the railroads; a measure to expand the authority of municipalities to manufacture their own power will awaken the greed of the private utility companies, and a mere bill to impose close controls or taxation on trading stamps is likely to ignite flaming interest on the part of the chain stores, some opposed, some not.

Such is the prevalence of the fetcher-bill technique that the most surprising thing about Paul Simon's article discussing it was that he had just discovered it. As an aspect of state legislative wealth, such behavior is as old as the Republic, and when Bryce wrote *The American Commonwealth*, a comprehensive study of the American state legislature, seventy-five years ago, he found it already had attained the perfection of an art. Enumerating various ways used by a legislator to make money, Bryce called this one "black-mailing," then explained: "A member brings in a bill ... directed against some particular great corporation ... or

to alter the general law ... to injure such a corporation. ...
He intimates privately that he is willing to 'see' the directors
or the law-agents of the corporations, and is in many cases
bought off. ...."

This technique of facilitating commercial intercourse
between the true constituency and the legislature is widely
regarded as evil. The observer should note that it cannot
occur without the clear acquiescence of the legislature. The
practitioner of it is identifiable by his behavior. For him to
succeed, it is necessary for all concerned to assume that (1)
the fetcher bill will not be dealt with on its merits and (2)
that legislative procedures, primarily the committee system,
will be used to deal with it in the desired way.

If the true constituency had any reason to believe that
a fetcher bill would be considered on its merits, it obviously
would have no incentive to play the fetcher-bill game with
one or two individuals. Because of the particular relationship of the true constituency and the legislature, however,
none of the parties involved holds any such belief.

So the fetcher-bill evil endures. Times have changed
since Bryce wrote, but not the state legislature.

16

★★★★★★★★★★★★★★★★★★★★★
★★★★★★★★★★★★★★★★★★★★★

"A PROVINCIAL LEGISLA-
TURE IS A FERTILE SOURCE
FOR A WRITER. SO MANY
CRIMES ARE COMMITTED
THERE DAILY IN AN ATMOS-
PHERE OF A SERVICE CLUB
SOCIAL, AND THE HUMAN
FLAWS ARE SO ACCESSIBLE.
SOMETIMES IT IS TOO MUCH
FOR ONE TO BEAR, THE MORE
OR LESS CONSTANT SPEC-
TACLE OF LEGISLATORS
BACKED BY THE SANCTION
OF POWERFUL BUSINESS
LOBBIES FRUSTRATING THE
FEW GOOD AND INTELLI-
GENT MEN WHO ARE WILL-
ING TO LABOR IN THE MAW
OF SMALL-TIME POLITICS."

—Willie Morris,
in *Commentary*

★★★★★★★★★★★★★★★★★★★★★
★★★★★★★★★★★★★★★★★★★★★

Corruption in the administra-
tive arm of state government springs from the same relationship as the legislature's internal corruption and is
broadly attributable to the legislature for several reasons.
A primary one is that the legislature is the author of the
statutes and codes that facilitate corrupt intercourse between the executive departments and the commercial community.

It is under the policies and by the administrative apparatus established by the legislature, for example, that

highway building programs are commonly tailored not on the basis of functional needs but to accommodate the commercial whims of the realty interests among others. Insurance departments and codes are commonly created by the legislature not to provide maximum protection to the purchaser of a policy but to assure that the regulatory department is a pliable cooperative instrumentality of the industry; it functions not so much to protect the people from the insurance industry as to insure that no serious competition occurs in this segment of the free-enterprise system. Similarly, the legislature is the author of those public construction programs that provide the most elaborate protections to the bond industry against suffering losses but almost no protection to the public against being gouged; at one preposterous extreme, the people in New York have yet to obtain a right to examine the books of several bond authorities, hence cannot discover whether they are being looted or not.

In Massachusetts a state crime commission spent three years, 1962 to 1965, looking at books and investigating the entire spectrum of state government. It found corruption almost everywhere it turned. Before it had even delivered its final report grand juries had indicted fifteen corporations and fifty-two individuals including more than a score of public officials past and present. Among them were a former governor, for bribery; two former house speakers, for bribery; and a former chairman of the house ways and means committee, for conflict of interest.

The commission found the usual varieties of corruption in the department of public works, the state housing board, the division of employment security, the food and drug division of the department of public health, the department of commerce, the turnpike authority, and, among others, the department of banking and insurance.

It was, curiously, in this latter department, the one that oversees the eminently genteel industry of banking, that the crime commission precipitated the most devastating number of indictments—at one blow nine corporations and twenty-one individuals including public officials and business executives. The commission reported a "pattern of corruption" as follows:

> Over a number of years bribes were paid to obtain small loan licenses, approvals of changes in names, changes in locations of small loan offices, transfers of ownership of small loan companies, and approvals for other transactions subject to regulation by the Bureau of Loan Agencies.

> In addition, bribes were paid to secure favorable action on legislation supported by the small loan industry or by certain companies within that industry. They were also paid to defeat legislation deemed adverse to the interests of the industry or of certain companies within the industry. The evidence indicates that the bribery was planned and accomplished through the control and misuse of a trade association, in part through informal planning and cooperation by the companies involved, and in part through individual action. Funds were obtained by various means, including the use of bills for legal services not rendered.

> Since the bribes amounted to substantial amounts, the companies paying them had to devise methods by which they would appear as deductible expenses. They also had to show the payments by check and at the same time obtain the money in cash for the bribes. Various means were used to accomplish these ends. Among them was the payment of fees to lawyers for non-existent services. The taxes were paid on the amounts received and, after deducting an honorarium, the balance was remitted to the company or to its designee.

> This entire pattern shows the extent to which an important segment of an industry can be victimized by corrupt officials and can become an active partner in a continuing program of bribery.

The report of the Massachusetts commission is more important than common journalistic assertions of legislative

corruption because nobody can scoff at it. The credentials of
the committee were top flight and its investigation was
painstaking and meticulous. Still, by and large, it only
documented what everybody already knew. Details of this
kind of corruption vary little from state to state. When Paul
Simon wrote about Illinois he might have been writing
about Massachusetts. With perhaps rare exceptions—of
which I have heard of none—the state legislature creates
policy and a governmental apparatus that is tuned to the
same intimate relationship with the commercial community
that exists within the legislature. To preach about this may
provide some emotional relief, but it is unlikely to alter it.

The Massachusetts crime commission saw very clearly
the culpability of the state legislature, the General Court, as
it is called there. The commission's comments on the
legislature were brief and are worth quoting for several
paragraphs because they not only reveal much about the
situation in Massachusetts but also illustrate a common inadequacy of conventional analysis. While the commission
had obtained mountains of evidence of the fruit of the legislature's links to the true constituency, it never perceived
this as the root of it all. It still tended to think of the legislature as the "direct link between the people and their
government" despite the fact that all the evidence dramatized a contrary truth. The observer is invited to note how
the commission's report is cast in terms of the conventional
doctrine about the composition of the legislature, how it
reflects a wistful wondering why the reality it found does
not coincide with the doctrine. The following few directly
quoted paragraphs may be uncommonly useful to the attentive observer:

> The authors of the State Constitution created the Legis-
> lature as one of three separate coequal branches of the
> state government. They armed the legislative branch
> with wide investigatory powers and charged it to enact
> such "orders, laws, statutes and ordinances, directions
> and instructions" as it deemed necessary for "the good
> and welfare of this commonwealth," thereby giving it

the power and duty to create an atmosphere of law, order and decency for the common good.

In the opinion of the Commission, the Legislature has failed in meeting this responsibility during the period covered by the Commission's investigations, and it must bear a major share of blame for the conditions in Massachusetts which made it necessary to create the Crime Commission.

While an official in high office, or groups in a department, may go astray without any instigation or assistance from the Legislature, it is inconceivable to the Commission that many of the members of the General Court were unaware of the corruption in our government.

Few have spoken out in protest. Those who have made efforts to remedy conditions were generally unable to muster the support necessary for success. Others who might have helped to improve the moral atmosphere did not do so for fear of losing the support of powerful members for their own legislative or political aims.

In the past, lack of moral backbone in the Legislature created an atmosphere that speeded the decline in the government.

Members of the Legislature are the direct link between the people and their government. The public must depend on the Legislature to take remedial action. When that responsibility is evaded or broken government is virtually out of control.

Some of the members of the Legislature have shown a conspicuous failure to maintain the independent attitude that is essential in taking legislative action for "the good and welfare of this Commonwealth."

For example, the names of a substantial number of legislators were found on payrolls of firms doing business directly or indirectly with the state.

Some of these legislators admitted that they had performed no services, or described services of such minor importance that the salaries paid could not be justified. Others who were on such payrolls refused to tell the Commission anything about the circumstances relating to payments to them.

The Legislature has ignored the separation of powers. It has interfered in the administration of the Executive Branch by insistence on patronage, by job freeze-ins, by direct control of various positions through its line budget procedure and by trades and deals forced on the Executive Branch in exchange for appropriations and legislation.

Such activities injure state employee morale, weaken the civil service system and contribute to the malfunctioning of state departments because of the ineptitude of patronage appointees.

The Commission has no recommendations for change in the legislative process. It must be obvious to all that inept or misdirected leadership, the annual volume of proposals, many of them yearly repeaters, and the last-minute confusion in clearing the docket have helped those with ulterior motive to gain their objectives.

The Commission recommends that a study be made of the legislative processes being followed in the General Court to determine whether some or all of the above conditions can be eliminated or minimized.

In 1966, studies of "legislative processes" were under way in at least thirty-two states including Massachusetts. Almost any casual newspaper reader can forecast the results of each of these surveys. First they will recommend that legislators receive more pay. After that, they will recommend better staffing, more office space, more orderly internal organization, longer sessions to provide more time for deliberation. They will recommend constitutional revisions to provide greater flexibility. Occasionally they will recommend tighter controls over lobbying, and they will often include a sermon on how the people should take greater interest in state government. None of these items, the observer will note, has any bearing on the cause of conditions that have led to all these studies.

The Massachusetts legislature, one of the better paid, has long recognized that high salaries are what it really needs. In fact, its first major action after the crime commission report set off a flurry of scandalized discussion was to enact a measure proposing a raise in its own pay.

The conventional lore naturally tends to dwell upon the more obvious and sensational instances of questionable behavior in and around the state legislature. It is easier to emphasize scandal than to delineate the deeper, subtler institutional corruption of the legislature.

Scandal also has the virtue of providing racy reading or listening.

One of the thigh-slappers that went the rounds in Tallahassee was about a pair of lobbyists who represented a segment of the financial industry. During each legislative session they maintained a stable of girls at a local hotel for the obvious business reasons. The story concerned the time one of the lobbyists forgot the business reasons and was helping himself to the company wares when his fellow lobbyist came into the room, saw what was going on, took a cane to his colleague's rump and roared an admonition that could be heard so well for such a distance that it became instant folklore.

"You get off that whore, Bill!" he yelled. "You know them whores is for the legislators!"

Such finely honed integrity is perhaps a rarity among lobbyists. Such lore is not. Lore about lobbyists has the ancient fascination of sin and sex simply because those are the universally present ingredients.

Out in California while one celebrated lobbyist was bragging, "I can tell if a man wants a baked potato, a girl or money," another lobbyist over in Montana was boasting, "Give me a case of scotch, a case of gin, one blonde, and one brunette and I can take any liberal," and—in the meantime —John Gunther was encountering in Austin, Texas, an ex-

pert who told him "that three B's control the legislature—
Bourbon, Beefsteak, Blondes."

There is no telling for sure how many variations have
been played on this "three B's" theme. In several state capitals they are said to stand for Bribes, Broads and Booze. No
matter.

The constant element in such lore is the intimation that
the state legislature meets in an aura of debauchery and is
thus corrupted. The intimation of debauchery is rooted in
fact, of course.

Yet the shortcoming of the conventional lore about it is
its failure to suggest that the sex-and-sin and wining-and-
dining traditions around the legislature are part of the ceremonial froth rather than an important cause of corruption.
The observer may understand this legislative folkway when
he perceives that it accomplishes two things apart from
creating a general spirit of camaraderie and conviviality.

One, by providing and financing lavish entertainment
(liquor, women, breakfasts, lunches, dinners, banquets,
balls), the true constituency establishes itself as the *host* at
the state capitol. It dramatizes its position as the well-spring
of bounty and power and affluence, and by casting the legislature in the role of guest it dramatizes through the social
charade the command which it exercises over the legislature
in other substantial ways.

Two, by accepting the role of *guest* the legislature similarly dramatizes its actual role as an intimate and affection-
ately subservient adjunct of the true constituency; at the
same time the legislature accepts the largesse as a pleasant
quid pro quo result of that relationship—much in the same
spirit that the country's corporate executives accept the
largesse of their high expense-account living as the bounty
due them from the stockholders. The relationship of the
legislature to the true constituency is not exactly that of the
executive corps to the stockholders but it is emotionally
comparable.

In the rounds of entertainment that occur during a legislative session it is possible, of course, that some outright

corruption results. That is, conceivably there has existed somewhere a legislator of such modest character that he would feel an obligation to vote a certain way as a result of accepting a baked potato, a bottle of whisky or a girl.

In general, however, the ceremonial debauchery merely dramatizes and reaffirms the relationship that has existed from time immemorial between the true constituency and the legislature. As well, the entertainment provides a sort of testing ground in which the true constituency can judge new legislators and decide how comfortably they will fit into the institutional partnership.

One utility company in Florida used to entertain numbers of legislators at a country lodge where a poker game was invariably started. Any new legislator who seemed to be losing heavily would be invited to take over the place—and bounteous stacks of chips—of a company minion who would find a reason to excuse himself. Obviously, the company could breathe easily about any legislator accepting the offer.

Similarly, the ceremonial debauchery tends to reduce generally the possibility of any pious and critical outcry when serious and practical corruption becomes necessary because of unforeseen events. Legislators who have been drinking gift whisky, eating gift food and sleeping with borrowed whores can afford to express only a certain amount of public moral indignation against the people who supplied it all. Still, this effect is incidental, merely additional insurance against possibilities of moral rebellion which have not over the years appeared to be excessively great in any state legislature.

The only legislative corruption that means anything in practical terms is lack of independence. As far as this country's society goes the institutional subservience of the legislature to the true constituency would not mean anything of itself; perhaps now, the way things have turned out, it does not actually make much difference at present. In any event, the only practical thing it has meant has been the historic neglect of public needs, the ultimate result of the fact that

the legislature has functioned as little more than a conduit
for the prevalent power of the true constituency. No matter
how fascinating they are, the stories of sex and sin tend to
becloud this truth about the essential corruption.

One example will illustrate. It is the case of Arthur H.
Samish.

In the 1940s Samish developed a reputation as one of
the most notorious and powerful lobbyists in the country.
His activities have been spread in the records of congressional committees and legislative committees and in the
mass press. They are solidly documented.

Samish was a Californian, a six-foot-two-inch, 300-
pound wheeler-dealer who was the author of one bit quoted
earlier. "I can tell if a man wants a baked potato, a girl or
money," he said.

Samish also had other things to say: "I'm the governor
of the legislature. To hell with the governor of the state. . . .
If you get a long enough ladder and put it up against the
Capitol dome, you can take a picture of me unscrewing the
gold cupola. . . ."

Things like that. Timidity was not his undoing.

Others had things to say about Samish, too. "Artie's the
real governor of California," said a prosperous corporation
lawyer. "The governor's only the Mikado. . . . Artie is the
Great Shogun."

Artie Samish operated under Governor Earl Warren,
and Warren was once asked, "Who has more influence with
the legislature, you or Artie Samish?"

"On matters that affect his clients," Warren replied.
"Artie unquestionably has more power than the governor."

Samish's clients at various times included companies
concerned with beer, liquor, motor buses, railroads, cigarettes, banks, building and loan companies, race tracks,
chemicals. "I represent industry," Samish would say in his
quieter moments. "I'm a lobbyist, a public relations man."

And this, in the end, was manifestly true. Samish developed an enormous reputation as a political genius, but it

was essentially an achievement of public relations. While he appeared to have developed immense personal power, scattering about campaign contributions and "electing" politicians and pushing bills through the legislature at will, he actually had only effectively identified himself with a broad spectrum of the true constituency.

After much public outrage, much of it triggered by an article about Samish by Lester Velie in *Collier's,* the California legislature voted to bar him "forever" from lobbying. Later Samish got in trouble with the courts, but neither that nor the legislature's action is important or to the point here.

Once Samish was barred and new lobbyist "control" laws were written there was a great sigh of relief as though everything had been improved.

Actually, nothing had changed. The true constituency had held the prevalent power before and the removal of Samish only meant that it would flow through different conduits.

In 1966, some seventeen years after the California legislature barred Samish, Governor Pat Brown talked about the situation in terms—not of power—but of "lobbyists."

"The lobbyists," Brown said, "will go along with you on social legislation. . . . But if you want to get a truth-in-lending bill or improve insurance laws or get rid of price fixing, well, they are much stronger than the governor. *I don't think the situation has really changed since Samish.* [Emphasis added.] Some interests today are stronger than they were in that era, and they have a great deal more money to spend than he ever had."

Corruption had not come to California as a result of Artie Samish or his baked potatoes, his money or his girls. It had come as a result of the true constituency's power and the legislature's response to it.

17

★★★★★★★★★★★★★★★★★★★★
★★★★★★★★★★★★★★★★★★★★

"THOSE WHO BEMOAN THE PASSING OF THE STATES SHED TEARS FOR THE LOSS OF POWER THAT HAD SCARCELY BEEN EXERCISED AND PROBABLY, IN THE NATURE OF THINGS, NEVER COULD HAVE BEEN ACTIVATED TO ANY MAJOR EXTENT."

—Key

★★★★★★★★★★★★★★★★★★★★
★★★★★★★★★★★★★★★★★★★★

In the tender years of my innocence one of my venerated editors used to offer me avuncular counsel about state politics.

"Remember," he would say, "venality is often preferable to stupidity."

I now agree.

And I have discovered that it is true that, insofar as one speaks of mere overt corruption, bribery and that sort of thing, one often is compelled to select one's heroes from among either the venal or the stupid.

Yet, to contemplate the deeper corruption of the legislature is to realize that there is not often such a clear opportunity of choice.

The corruption of identity, the corruption of legislative independence, the corruption of power has produced an institutional corruption of mind that is likely to strike the observer not as stupidity so much as some form of atrophy. It impresses nearly every firsthand observer. Wyoming journalist Olga Moore spoke of the "look of consecrated negativism" about a legislator. Florida newsman Robert Delaney once was inspired to speak of a legislator who sounded "like a Demosthenes who has lost his pebbles." The impression is not one of outright lunacy so much as some kind of aridity. Down in Texas *Harper's* editor Willie Morris recalled an old-timer who had concluded that the legislature "cared as much about intellectual enlightenment as a razorback sow about Keats's 'Ode on a Grecian Urn.' " To two Michigan State University political scientists, Charles Press and Charles R. Adrian, writing on "Why Our State Governments Are Sick" in the Summer '64 *Antioch Review*, it seemed that "most contemporary state legislatures have inherited the discarded mantle and way of thinking of the pre-1937 Supreme Court." A group of some eighty students of state government who convened at Columbia University's 1966 American Assembly in New York issued a statement that said state government has been handicapped, among other reasons, "because legislators themselves have been unduly timid in using the powers they already possess to strengthen their roles." Such comments on the viability of the legislative mind are neither novel nor new. Seventy-five years ago Bryce noted: "Nothing is more remarkable about these State legislators than their timidity. No one seems to think of having an opinion of his own."

What has happened in the broadest sense is that in the role of minion to the true constituency's power the state legislature has developed the almost sparkless mentality that is common to serfdom everywhere. From this springs the habitual anxiety that one finds among state politicians over the "loss" of state power.

It is really an inversion of anxieties spawned by a vague awareness of unused power, unflexed authority. It is the curse of minionhood. The legislature has largely foreclosed its own power, thwarted its own volition, in favor of functioning as a channel for the true constituency's power. The dearth of legislative creativity is but a corollary result of this.

In the conventional lore a broad miscellany of practices has been cited as reasons for this legislative characteristic, this want of creativity. Yet, while disagreeing on causes, students and critics invariably recognize the condition. "The underlying pattern of state government is as monotonous as the gridiron layout of city streets," said Arthur W. Bromage in *State Government and Administration in the United States*. "The inventive genius that characterizes American private affairs does not penetrate the structure of state government."

As he suggests, it is not surprising that such a trait should stick out so in a society that has all but made a cult of innovation and experimentation. Neither is it surprising that in this mobile society critics nearly invariably turn to automotive concepts for the figures of speech with which to suggest legislative atrophy. It has been written seemingly millions of times, for instance, that the legislature is equipped for "the horse-and-buggy days" when it needs the equipment to solve "space-age" or "jet-age" problems. One handicap usually cited is the "horse-and-buggy" state constitution.

It would have been difficult for even a beginning observer to have escaped these mataphors. They have been dusted off and trotted out or revved up in every state of the union except Hawaii and Alaska. Save for some fear of seeming anachronistic, a critic might fittingly use them in those new states, simply because their legislatures at creation assumed, as though by osmosis, the institutional characteristics observable in state legislatures everywhere. Admittedly it might seem bizarre to speak of Alaska's new legislature as a relic of the "horse-and-buggy" days.

The figure of speech has disadvantages in all cases, however. It clearly carries an implication that the legislature was at one time fitted to do a proper job, to match the tempo of the era, to stay in tune with the rhythms of society. By implication, the conventional metaphoricians would convince us that the state legislature performed okay back when the horse-and-buggy days were still at hand. That is what they were equipped for, the supposition is.

The truth is that the legislative atrophy has been a continuing characteristic. The enormous lag between the workings of its institutional mind and society's has been ever noticeable. To discover this one need only turn to the commentary that was being produced *during* the horse-and-buggy days, of which the following is a sample:

". . . We seem entirely oblivious to the forward strides of our republic. . . . We seem to forget that, since the days of the first thirteen states, our population and social and economic conditions have undergone wonderful changes. Then society was agricultural and wealth individual; now society is urban and wealth corporate. The change in needs and the multiplicity and diversity of emergencies which arise in this complex society we meet with the legislative methods which were suited to the simple needs of a sparsely settled agricultural community."

That was written in 1904. It was a piece about "Our State Legislatures" by Samuel P. Orth in the *Atlantic Monthly*.

"Under enormously changed conditions," wrote A. E. Buck a generation later, in 1936, "both socially and governmentally, which have developed with increasing tempo since the World War, we are still trying to struggle along with a state legislative system that belongs essentially *to the stagecoach era*." (My emphasis.) Buck wrote a pamphlet, *Modernizing Our State Legislatures,* put out by the American Academy of Political and Social Science.

In 1965, a generation after that, free-lance writer James Nathan Miller toured the country, observed several legislatures, and in a National Municipal League pamphlet expressed his own conclusion that their "horse-and-buggy methods are clearly identifiable and can be remedied." He added: "Ironically, the remedy involves divorcing ourselves from the theories of one of our greatest political philosophers, Thomas Jefferson. For it is Jefferson's dream of a simple agrarian society that today haunts operations of state legislatures." I dissent.

Inevitably, like every other contemporary critic who writes on this subject, Miller quoted Charles S. Rhyne, the former American Bar Association president who argued the big reapportionment case before the Supreme Court. As

Rhyne put it: "Internally, the legislatures remain as archaic as before. They continue to try to solve jet-age problems with horse-and-buggy methods and, in their failure to do it, they're digging their own graves and inviting federal intervention." Neatly said.

Each contemporary critic, in his day, seems to assume that the state legislature would perform in a modern, efficient, spiffy way if it would simply turn in its old forms for new ones. This habit of thought is undoubtedly a by-product of Detroit. If there were just a "streamlined" constitution, as is so often said, why the legislature would just swoosh along keeping right up with the rest of the traffic in the American mainstream.

What such hopeful critics and students tend to overlook is that the state legislature's lag is a result of its institutional mind and not the result of its equipment. The equipment, of course, is the product of the same mind, and its general obsolescence is only more testimony to the quality and inhibitions of the mind.

As to such equipment as the state constitution and the possibilities of "streamlining" it, what one discovers in practice is that when a legislature undertakes revision it alters the language but makes no substantial changes except in the superstructure of government; it may realign a few executive departments, which is hardly relevant to what ails the state. A new constitution, when actually written by a legislature, invariably contains the same organic deficiencies that made it appear to be a "horse-and-buggy" constitution in the first place. When a state convention rewrites a constitution it will be observed that state legislators and politicians with a state legislative frame of mind dominate it, and the result is the same. Michigan, for example, had barely stopped cheering over its brand new constitution, one that George Romney took credit for steering through, when it was discovered that it contained the same financial restrictions that were the only real disadvantage of the old one. The new constitution flatly rejected graduated income taxation.

Everybody has taken note of the extensive restrictions

on legislative power contained in state constitutions. They read usually like detailed statutes. They set salaries and establish regulatory commissions and earmark some taxes while proscribing others. Many, many theoreticians advance the belief that these restrictions reflect the distrust of the people toward the legislature—the idea being that since the people approve the constitutions in referenda the contents reflect their will. This is largely poppycock. For one thing, the people have historically been indifferent to such constitutional referenda. In 1965 when Connecticut voted on several important new provisions hardly a fifth of the voters bothered to cast a ballot. For another, it is an observable fact that the resistance to removing the restrictions is centered within the legislature and within a leadership that shares its frame of mind. The restrictions on taxation, after all, only protect the true constituency. And so do those many provisions that make regulatory agencies and commissions constitutional rather than statutory bodies. With their potency curtailed in the constitution there is less danger that they can be strengthened by statute.

I personally watched four or five different committees and commissions rewrite Florida's state constitution in different ways without ever altering any of the substantial organic provisions that made the old one undesirable. The legislature constructs these documents—or sees to their construction—not to provide flexible government that might effectuate the will of the people but to provide safeguards for the true constituency against the exercise of that popular will.

The legislature's success in achieving this is, of course, reflected by the condition already noted: the disenchantment of the people in state government and their reliance on the federal for the new practical programs that will help the society to develop.

Meanwhile, the state legislature continues to sense a "loss" of power without ever realizing what the trouble is. The most common complaint, naturally, is that the state power has been "grabbed" by Washington. There is a companion theory that the legislature's power has "drifted" to the executive branch. In 1961 the final report of the National Legislative Conference's committee on legislative processes and procedures said this: "The drift or shift of power from the legislative branch has slowed and to some extent reversed in recent years. Conscious, concerted, and continuing effort will be required, however, before the balance is redressed, particularly in the light of the tremendous expansion in the *business* [gratuitous emphasis] of state government in this century. Opposition can be anticipated. . . . The electorate is *likely to be apathetic* [gratuitous emphasis] unless the purpose and objectives of change are made crystal clear."

In that report, by chance, the National Legislative Conference called for longer sessions, longer legislative terms, bigger pay, bigger staffs, reorganization of committees and, among other things, the adoption of "modern techniques."

These things, it was presumed, would increase the legislature's "power."

It is not necessary to belabor metaphysical distinctions between the various aspects of power, but the observer may find it helpful to be reminded that for the most part these notes and comments do not pertain to the prime power of the people. They pertain mostly to governmental power, the capacity to make law.

The references to the power of the true constituency are obviously to economic power that the true constituency has no difficulty translating into governmental power through the state legislature.

Most of the time the prime power of the people remains quiescent in spite of all the activity that involves governmental power. The government functions under powers sometimes consciously delegated by the people. Sometimes the people simply delegate by acquiescence. They retain in all cases their prime power which is simply the capacity to turn things upside down if they get too bad. Mostly, the people are long-suffering, but from Shays' Rebellion to the Watts riots they demonstrate from time to time that their patience has limits. A brief excursion into the subject of power may help remove some misunderstandings.

When the legislature complains of a loss of power it does not mean that the people of the state have lost power, as they obviously have not. When the states' righter complains that the state has lost power, he tries to intimate that the people of the state have lost power, but instinctively, of course, the people know better. They retain the prime power.

As to governmental power the people have demonstrated in a long series of national elections that they will have it exercised by Washington after having concluded that the state legislature will not use it. Meanwhile, the people's prime power remains quiescent except in times of extraordinary stress. Regimes come and go at the state-house without affecting it.

An extreme case will provide a clearer illustration. Take the regime of Huey Long in Louisiana. It is well documented that he became a dictator over the governmental affairs of the state. Yet in doing this he did not have to take power away from the people. Huey Long wrenched power away from the Standard Oil Company and a coalition of other commercial entities that held it prior to his assumption of office—the true constituency of the time. The Louisiana legislature suddenly discovered that Huey Long was its true constituency or—more accurately—the sole conduit between it and the true constituency that was the commercial community.

The legislators now served Huey Long instead of Standard Oil. Many Americans were shocked when Long publicly boasted that he could buy legislators "like bags of potatoes." It should not have been surprising. The true constituency had been buying them for generations.

Prior to Huey Long the legislature's power was exercised almost exclusively in the interests of the commercial community. Long exercised it partly in his own interest but also generously in the interest of the people.

"The people of Louisiana got a state government which did more for them than any other government in Louisiana's history," said Schlesinger in *Politics of Upheaval.* "The power of the *oligarchy* [my emphasis], which had for so long sucked the people dry, was now broken." Long exercised legislative power to build schools and provide free texts where there had been none, to construct roads where mud tracks had run, to expand hospitals and public services generally.

His methods outraged many Americans because they seemed to conflict with deeply held ideals. Actually, he was using the same methods used universally by the true constituency—but for different purposes. Through forceful politics and shrewd public relations he became the sole conduit between the true constituency and the legislature. On a smaller scale lobbyist Artie Samish did the same in California and developed his reputation for possessing more power than the governor. Samish was also described as a dictator over the legislature.

In none of Huey Long's operations did the people of Louisiana actually lose their prime power. The Long revolution took the form of a transition of power that had long since passed from the people's hands, some of it by constitutional delegation and some of it by acquiescence. After Huey Long was assassinated one backwoods Louisiana peckerwood summarized the difference in the way power had been used by the true constituency prior to Long. "Before Huey Long," he said, "we didn't have anything. Now we at least have something. That's the difference."

Huey Long is discussed here not to raise an argument over the rightness of his political actions or the wrongness of his skullduggery. My point is not to offer a moral lesson but to clarify some notions of power that tend to get confused in many discussions.

Another useful illustration occurs in the Virginia that has existed under Harry Byrd, former governor and until recently a United States senator. From the 1920s until the 1960s Byrd was the genteel dictator in Virginia and differed from Huey Long primarily in his facade and his aims. Both rose to power by virtue of their considerable personalities and adroitness but in different ways. Long wrested power away from the true constituency. Byrd's ascendancy may be attributed to the fact that his interests were synonymous with the true constituency's.

The true constituency never had to contest Byrd's ascension because there was never any danger that he would dictate any state action contrary to the commercial community's general wishes. He never disappointed them but once, and it was at that time that the true constituency cut him down. That later. For the most part, Byrd used his power to assure that the government did as little as possible for the people. Harry Byrd was ever more genteel than Huey Long but never half as humanitarian.

While Long at length began to tamper with elections like a banana republic despot, the Virginia government under Byrd's control has for generations methodically enforced an election code that has reduced the active electorate in the state to the smallest in the nation at times. With this small and tightly controlled electorate Byrd never had to buy legislators like sacks of potatoes because he owned the preponderance of them at the time of their designation.

Nor did Byrd ever have to tamper with the judiciary or school administrations as Huey Long did, simply because under a "model" constitution that crowned Byrd's administration as governor, the legislature selects all the circuit judges and the judges appoint the electoral boards that appoint the school boards. Byrd, of course, more or less appointed the legislature and controlled it to such an extent that in the 1950s when some young members sought to make it behave independently the newspapers called it the Rebellion of the Young Turks. For the most part, when Byrd said "camel" the General Assembly tended to hump. He picked the governors and remained, himself, the primary constituency of the state legislature, the single conduit between it and the true constituency.

The fact that Byrd's power finally was only synonymous with that of the true constituency's was illustrated on the one occasion when it chose to intercede on its own behalf. This came at the conclusion of the experiment known as Massive Resistance, which Byrd had dictated. In brief, the segregationist fulminations were beginning to hurt Virginia economically to the extent that the commercial community wished to change the course of state policy. Byrd was not ready to give up, however, and therefore neither was Governor J. Lindsay Almond. However, the true constituency at length decided to pull the rug. Twenty-nine corporate executives—businessmen, industrialists, bankers —invited Almond to dinner at the Rotunda Club in Richmond.

Benjamin Muse, the historian of Massive Resistance, summarized the nature of the meeting: "No one said in so many words: 'This nonsense has gone far enough,' but the state's business leaders expressed their urgent concern." The result, shortly, was the end of Massive Resistance. Almond capitulated, so did the legislature, and Byrd's power began to fade precipitately. The true constituency had come briefly into its own. Byrd's minions revealed the depth of their chagrin by denouncing Almond as a turncoat. All that had happened, however, was that Almond became subject to and transmitted to the legislature the same power that Harry Byrd had been transmitting all along.

None of this is to raise moral questions about the behavior of Harry Byrd, whose gentility has always glowed like a well-polished winesap. This merely illustrates the way that great events happen in state government with no particular reference to the prime power of the people.

18

★★★★★★★★★★★★★★★★★★★★
★★★★★★★★★★★★★★★★★★★★

"THE POLICY-MAKING POWER
OF INDUSTRIAL EXECUTIVES,
TO CITE JUST ONE GROUP, IS
PROBABLY CONSIDERABLY
GREATER IN NATIONAL AF-
FAIRS THAN THE COMBINED
STRENGTH OF STATE GOV-
ERNORS."

—Glenn E. Brooks,
When Governors Convene

★★★★★★★★★★★★★★★★★★★★
★★★★★★★★★★★★★★★★★★★★

The state legislature suffers from the impotence of its own subservience to the true constituency. Obviously, it *could*, granted the will, govern the true constituency instead of vice versa.

The weakness suffered by American governors is something different. Often they are more or less mandated to do great things. But few of them possess the personal force, the wit or will to interpose themselves between the true constituency and the legislature. The result is that they experience an impotence that they commonly attribute to the legislature. Huey Longs have been rare, and in general American governors have either not sought to or have been unable to tap the real power that exists in the states.

A few, of course, have tried valiantly to overwhelm the true constituency. In the early 1930s Floyd Bjornstjerne Olson developed a reputation as a formidable radical leader while governor of Minnesota. With great force and flamboyance he recommended a state income tax, public power, unemployment insurance and programs of mortgage assistance. As it turned out, his rhetoric was more formidable than he. The legislature scrapped most of his program. The true constituency controlled.

The example of Soapy Williams of Michigan, already cited, is similar. Williams did bulldoze many public improvements through the legislature, but the superior power of the true constituency revealed itself when he reached repeated stalemates on methods of financing. In California both Earl Warren and Pat Brown have been known as "strong" and socially progressive governors—and each has admitted the superior power within the legislature of the true constituency. In 1966 Governor Richard Hughes of New Jersey discovered that his overwhelming popular mandate and his party's new superiority in the legislature had no bearing on the chances of his fiscal program. The legislature's actions spring neither from the party nor the people but from the true constituency, and the only time the governor succeeds with substantial programs is when he has found ways to command the true constituency or when he is serving it.

It would be foolish not to suppose that much of Nelson Rockefeller's success as a "strong" governor in New York results not so much from his unusually broad constitutional powers as from the fact that he has quite a good friend at Chase Manhattan. His family practically invented the true constituency and, like Byrd, he is practically synonymous with it. Unlike Byrd, he is humanitarian, a fortunate side effect in America of learning how to spend unneeded millions.

It has been fashionable to applaud William Scranton as a successful "strong" governor of Pennsylvania. He was widely applauded for obtaining a legislative victory in revising an unemployment compensation law—expanding benefits for the "deserving" unemployed. It should be seen, however, that his revision was not offensive to the true constituency and that, in most ways, Scranton has run an austerity administration, by his own testimony. As for his general success with the legislature, here are some things Scranton himself pointed out at the start of the 1966 session:

Despite the clear need for Constitutional revision the legislature passed only half of the essential amendments that were recommended by the Commission on Constitutional Revision.

Despite the rising toll of accidents on our highways and the dangerous presence of crime in our urban communities, the House . . . killed in committee both a bill that would have authorized an expanded complement for our State Police and a bill setting up a new Department of Public Safety.

Despite the availability of $3 million in Federal funds for help in beautification of our highways, the Legislature did not act finally on legislation that would have made receipt of these funds possible.

Despite the clear and present danger to many home owners from coal mine subsidence in the bituminous region, and from insufficiently regulated strip mining in the anthracite region, the legislature failed to provide cures to either of these problems.

Despite evidence that fraud continues to be practiced at polling places in some parts of Pennsylvania on every election day, a bill containing reforms in our election laws was watered down and finally killed on the last day of the session.

Et cetera. All this hardly reflected Byrd-like or Long-like or even Rockefeller-like command over the legislature. What Scranton appeared most proud of in that 1966 address was the fact that the state was now making more loans than ever to industry.

In this, the legislature had cooperated. It broadened the Pennsylvania Industrial Development Authority, and Scranton cheered that "more PIDA loans—both in number and amount—have been made in the past three years than in the entire prior six years of PIDA's existence." Scranton also boasted that a record $105-million surplus "did not lead us to abandon our policy of governmental austerity. . . ." In this, too, Scranton found the legislature sympathetic.

A few weeks later, however, speaking to the New York Chamber of Commerce, Scranton was giving voice to the same feelings of impotence that governors everywhere experience. He said that state governments have been left "in the position of frustrated bystanders" and he called state government "the sleeping giant of the past few decades."

This, too, is hardly the talk of a man who feels that he has been flexing the power of the state. And, of course, he had not.

This feeling of impotence—or somnolence—is simply the ultimate result of the dominion of the true constituency over the legislature. Though American governors are obliged to crow over petty victories they have long since perceived the near impossibility of marshaling the real force of the state government. At some times they speak of the loss of power. The truth seems to be that they have despaired at ever tapping into that power.

Early in this century when the governors first gathered in what grew to be the national Governors Conference, they talked endlessly about the need for new credit facilities for farmers—a need then already evident. They did nothing, however, except watch the national government enact the Federal Farm Loan Act in 1916.

Such was the behavior of the governors conferring that by 1927 when they convened at Mackinac Island, Michigan, the *Chicago Daily News* hailed the deliberations as "The Governors Annual Frolic." In a slim useful volume called *When Governors Convene,* Glenn E. Brooks pointed out that when the Depression struck "the inability—or unwillingness—of the governors to close their ranks for decisive action was cause for serious concern about the leadership of the state chief executives. A Governors' Conference that could not muster the authority to act in the face of bread lines was no longer a matter for humorous criticism." Brooks pointed out that the conference of 1931 ruled out every subject of critical national concern. Instead, the governors discussed—extradition.

Actually, it is fairer to conclude that the governors' seeming lack of leadership reflected not so much dull minds as a conviction that the state legislatures could not be brought to action. There is some documentation for this interpretation. During the New Deal a countrywide poll was taken of governors asking them whether the states should take over the relief programs. Only one governor said that it should be handled by the states. That governor, Gene Talmadge of Georgia, had already distinguished himself by declaring at his inaugural: "The only way to have an honest government is to keep it poor. You can't help the people by giving them something. You weaken their soul and their heart, and dry up their muscles." What about the unemployed, Talmadge was asked. "Let 'em starve," he said. Talmadge did sponsor a widely publicized retrenchment policy that included a broad reduction in property taxes. The reduction saved the average Georgia farmer fifty-three cents while saving millions for the Georgia Power Company. Talmadge had great power in the legislature.

In spite of their rhetoric, governors generally today demonstrate no greater confidence than then in the capacity of the states. Eisenhower, naively perhaps, put them to the test several times. He held, as he told the Governors Conference of 1953, an "indestructible conviction that unless we preserve in this country the place of the state government . . . then we are not going to have an America as we have known it. . . ." It was in 1959 that Eisenhower asked the governors to obtain greater state payments to the unemployed to avoid further national action. The result? A statement that applauded Eisenhower's belief that the states should retain responsibility for jobless benefits—without mentioning his request for an increase in state benefits. Eisenhower's administration, too, proposed state participation in a grant-in-aid medical care program. The 1960 Governors Conference resolved—30 to 13—to reject the federal-state plan in favor of a national program.

This surprised no one familiar with the gubernatorial response to Eisenhower's proposal that the states take over certain taxing functions exercised by the federal government. It was Ike who established a "Joint Federal-State Action Committee" with this purpose: "To designate functions which the states are ready and willing to assume and finance that are now performed or financed wholly or in part by the federal government. . . . To recommend the federal and state revenue adjustments required to enable the states to assume such functions. . . . To identify functions and responsibilities likely to require state or federal attention in the future. . . ."

Out of a thick report came one recommendation that may be worth mentioning: that the U.S. allow the states to enact a tax on local telephone service up to 40 per cent of the federal tax. Governor Orville L. Freeman of Minnesota summed up the impact of the federal-state action committee. Its recommendations, he said, "have failed to generate any enthusiasm among the Governors, or, for that matter anyone else—the White House, Congress, state legislators or public groups. In fact, the most notable aspect of the report is the heavy silence that has followed its release."

These few examples merely expose the fundamental disenchantment of the governors with the state legislature. Long experience has spawned the sense of impotency among the governors. They retain no real belief that they can tap substantially into the power exercised over the legislature. Only in rare instances can governors of extraordinary personal force do so.

19

So far I have suggested that the relationship between the true constituency and the legislature accounts for its alienation, its corruption, its feeling of power lost, its loss of relevancy within the national system, its loss of relevancy to the people.

Here I also suggest that it indirectly accounts for the state legislature's obsession with trivia—its chronic affliction by that ailment that I call *microphilia.*

An individual whose main powers are thwarted or blocked in some way often develops a compulsive or obsessive preoccupation with irrelevant trivia. Psychologists recognize an individual's compulsive, lint-picking fastidousness as a symptom of inhibited mental powers or distorted emotional powers. Case histories reveal that such persons, instead of coping with real problems that suddenly confront them, will turn to dusting books, rearranging phonograph records, or they will manicure their nails or repeatedly shampoo their hair. In so doing they convince themselves of their own busy-ness while distracting themselves from the problems they feel ill equipped to encounter. Compulsive trivial activity thus preserves them from a destructive and overwhelming comprehension of their own inadequacy.

In the vast majority of its actions the state legislature appears to be behaving in a strikingly similar way. Microphilia is perennially and universally evident in the statehouse.

Reporters and scholars occasionally try to convey an

idea of the amount of the trivia that occupies a state legislature's days. "U.S. legislatures," said *Newsweek,* "cannot be faulted on quantity. Legislators, some 7,800 in all, generate a floodtide of roughly 112,000 pieces of legislation every two years. The sheer mass of bills is impressive; the frenetic processing of them is awe-inspiring. But the fruits of hyperkinetic legislative labor often inspire more wonder than awe. In little Montpelier, Vt., lawmakers use up vast energies fighting over whether to ban non-returnable beer bottles." The story went on to note that after wrangling for twenty-nine days over a party leadership question, New York's 1965 Assembly finally enacted its first bill with this earthshaking title: "An Act to Amend the Code of Criminal Procedure, in Relation to the Appointment of Grand Jury Stenographers in Saratoga County."

In truth, there is no way adequately to summarize the experience of witnessing 7,800 legislative microphiliacs in action. The impression that one gains sitting through months and months of sessions is not easily conveyed. To say that the legislature is bogged down in trivia is to say nothing close to the truth.

It is more than bogged down; it compulsively wallows in trivia; it is a fountain of trivia, issuing forth an innundation of trivia at every session. To witness it day after day is to disbelieve it. The very notion that the lawmaking body of a state should so occupy itself is preposterous.

Still, it is true that the observer learns many lessons by keeping tabs on the trivia. It is through this that he sees the legislature so frequently belie its own image of itself. It believes in government closest to the people—yet retains control of the salary of the common clerks of the lowest courts. It believes in free enterprise—yet prescribes in minutest detail the equipment to be used by barbers, the shape of the box that grapefruit must be packed in. A champion of liberty, it prescribes minutely how students are to be oriented and brainwashed. Once, in 1923, New Hampshire's legislature even received a bill to regulate the hours of sleep ("eight out of each twenty-four hours shall be the minimum time for sleep"). Unaccountably, it did not pass.

I have decided that there is no way to comprehend this legislative obsession, this microphilia, without witnessing it. It is conveyed in neither newspapers nor magazines because there simply is not space. But I have selected fewer than a hundred bills passed by the California legislature in 1965. They were selected at random from a summary digest published by the state. The reader may scan them not at all, or rapidly, or give them passing study. I suggest at least passing study, for laughs if nothing else, and the observer should try to imagine these laws flowing by the tens of thousands from every legislature in the land. The samples follow, a list of acts in which the California legislature wrote new laws to:

1. Add Route 261, from Route 101 near Longvale to Route 5 near Willows via vicinity of Covelo and Mendocino Pass, to state highway system.

2. Exclude rubbish or garbage truck while actually engaged in collection of rubbish or garbage within business or residence district from requirements of various Vehicle Code sections regulating operation and parking of motor vehicles.

3. Require, when grapefruit is distributed or sold in bags which have a net content of not more than 25 pounds per bag, that bags be placed in closed standard container number 62, except when only one bag is mailed, delivered or sold directly to consumer.

4. Prescribe requirements and tolerances for new standard container number 62 and define term "closed" when applied to such container.

5. Provide that whenever the legislative body of any city determines on the basis of engineering and traffic survey that prima facie speed limit of 25 miles per hour in business or residential district on any roadway not exceeding 25 feet in width, other than a state highway, is more than reasonable or safe, such legislative body may by ordinance determine and declare prima facie speed limit of 20

or 15 miles per hour, whichever is found most appropriate and is reasonable and safe.

6. Include Mariposa and Mono Counties in the state teletype system.

7. Raise the salary of the Mono County auditor from $7,200 to $8,400 and the district attorney's salary from $6,200 to $12,480, and prohibit the district attorney from engaging in private practice of law during his term of office.

8. Require the department of parks and recreation to provide for the preservation, development and interpretation of grounds upon which Bidwell Mansion is located, rather than to limit preservation, development, and interpretation to Bidwell Mansion.

9. Add new branch to professional engineering designated as "metallurgical engineering," and provide that state board of registration for civil and professional engineers may register without examination applicant in that branch who files application not later than June 30, 1966, provided applicant has all qualifications necessary for such registration.

10. Provide that cattle brand is prima facie evidence owner of brand was owner of cattle, and that right to use brand is established by copy of filing made with bureau of livestock identification.

11. Make it unlawful for registered owner or driver, if such owner is not then present, to aid or abet in littering of highways.

12. Provide that a member of the senate or assembly who is not returned to office following a reapportionment of his legislative district may retire under Legislators' Retirement System (LRS), without regard to age, provided he is credited with at least four years' service.

13. Require a prescription and physician's report for the procurement of any cough syrup or cough medicine containing codeine, but allow the dispensing of such cough syrup or cough medicine on oral order, which shall be reduced to writing with 24 hours.

14. Prohibit a pedestrian from suddenly leaving a curb or other place of safety and walking or running into the path of a vehicle so close as to constitute an immediate hazard.

15. Provide that the prohibition against the sale of alcoholic beverages near certain institutions does not apply to any bona fide club meeting specified requirements located within 2,000 feet of San Quentin Prison.

16. Authorize public cemetery districts to cause to be purchased and erected markers upon graves of indigents and to accept gifts or donations to purchase or erect grave markers, but limit such expenditures to $20 per grave, such provisions to remain in effect until October 1, 1971.

17. Extend from the 91st day after adjournment of the 1965 Regular Session to the 91st day after adjournment of the 1967 Regular Session provisions making yellow-billed magpies (Pica nuttalli) nonprotected birds in counties where boards of supervisors resolve that nonprotection is desirable because of crop damage.

18. Include leases for growing asparagus among those leases which are excepted from the 10-year limitation on leases which may receive probate court approval.

19. Permit the board of barber examiners to contract or otherwise arrange for reasonably required physical accommodations and facilities to conduct examinations.

20. Permit director of fish and game, or his representative, to grant, without hearing or notice, to fish reduction plants a license to dispose of dead or dying fish whenever it is determined that an emergency situation exists.

21. Relax prohibition against transporting striped bass into or out of the state to permit sportfishing licensees of California and Arizona lawfully taking fish from the Colorado River on water or on shore of the other state to transport the fish into Arizona or California, respectively.

22. Provide that native gold is the official state mineral and serpentine the state rock.

23. Increase from 20 to 25 years the maximum period for which commercial or savings banks may make loans on

security of first lien on real property and specified leaseholds and to increase the maximum amount of such loans from 75 to 80 per cent of market value of such property.

24. Permit the director of the Youth Authority to designated a qualified officer of his department as his representative at meetings of the Youth Authority Board for an indefinite period of time in the future, instead of only until October 1, 1965.

25. Make county administrative officer an officer of county.

26. Permit elementary school pupils living in territory of specified elementary school district which was divided and included in unified district, as a result of latter's formation, to attend elementary school which pupils would have normally attended had such unified district not been formed where unified district does not maintain an elementary school in such included territory.

27. Reduce from 36 to 31 the number of states within which an American national fraternal organization must operate, and from 500 to 300 the number of units which such an organization must operate, in order to qualify as a club for purpose of Alcoholic Beverage Control Act.

28. Provide for administrative regulations for loading and transportation of empty wooden boxes.

29. Extend until January 1, 1968, the time in which persons meeting specified requirements may obtain psychiatric technicians certificate without examination, increase the renewal fee to not more than $15 and provide that the Psychiatric Technicians Law shall become inoperative on January 1, 1968, if revenues are insufficient to pay for expenses incurred in its operation.

30. Change the name of highway transportation agency and administrator of highway transportation to transportation agency and administrator of transportation, respectively.

31. Prohibit title insurers, controlled escrow companies and others selling evidence of title to real property from paying for or offering to pay for or furnishing any advertis-

ing to the customer in connection with the sale of real property interests.

32. Increase the number of judges in Oakland-Piedmont Judicial District from nine to ten, and in San Leandro-Hayward Judicial District from two to three.

33. Require department of California highway patrol to adopt regulations relating to standards and certification procedure for new tires of passenger vehicle type, as it determines necessary to provide for public safety, and to prohibit selling passenger vehicle tires not in compliance with the regulations and to except motorcycles and housecars from the above provisions.

34. Change measurement to be used in determining minimum size of crabs that may be taken for commercial purposes from seven inches, measured across back from point to point, to six and one-quarter inches, measured by the shortest distance through the body from edge of shell to edge of shell directly from front of points.

35. Authorize a Santa Barbara County supervisor to use his own car or a county automobile when traveling on official business requiring automobile travel and to allow mileage if he elects to use his own car for all such traveling.

36. Prescribe standards for melon crates 44H, 44I, 44J and 44K, and require all melons, except cantaloupes and watermelons, to be packed in such containers, with specified exceptions.

37. Provide for appointment of official court reporter for Calaveras County Superior Court.

38. Revise standards, markings and containers for tangerines, mandarins, oranges, lemons and grapefruit.

39. Authorize local health officer, with the approval of the governing body of jurisdiction for which he acts, to destroy duplicate and triplicate copies of reports of premarital and prenatal blood tests which have been retained two years or longer.

40. Change the name of the County Livestock Inspector to County Veterinarian.

41. Authorize the insurance commissioner to make cor-

rections, within six months following his original action, in any record, finding, determination, order, rule or regulation made by him, if he is satisfied that it is just to do so and that such material would have contained such a correction but for mistake, clerical error, inadvertence, surprise or excusable neglect.

42. Include dental operations upon an animal within the practice of veterinary medicine.

43. Modify provisions respecting classes of persons to whom yacht and ship brokers commission may issue licenses.

44. Provide that, prior to construction of new court facilities, the board of supervisors shall submit proposed plans to the judge or judges of the affected court for review and recommendation and that review and recommendation shall not be disregarded without reasonable grounds.

45. Permit importation into the state of black marlin (Makaira indica) for the purpose of manufacturing fish cakes for human consumption.

46. Require that egg products be prepared only from eggs fit for human consumption.

47. Recast definitions of mobile home and camp car for purposes of laws re mobile homes and mobile-home parks, and to add definitions of self-contained mobile home, trailer coach and travel trailer.

48. Create an advisory commission on the status of women, consisting of 15 members: three from the senate, appointed by the rules committee, three from the assembly, appointed by the speaker, the superintendent of public instruction, the chief of the division of industrial welfare in the department of industrial relations, and seven public members appointed by the governor with the consent of the senate; and authorize the commission to study the status of women in various fields and to have its own advisory committee, and require it to report its findings and recommendations to the legislature not later than the fifth legislative day of the 1967 Regular Session, and to appropriate $35,000 for these purposes.

49. Require that when a weighmaster is weighing any earthmoving vehicle for purposes of weight certification, when such vehicle is being used in connection with a construction project, tare weight of the vehicle or the gross weight of the vehicle and its contents shall be determined with the driver in the vehicle and include his weight.

50. Exempt casaba melons shipped intrastate from provisions establishing standard containers for melons.

51. Permit governor to make Governor's Award, consisting of a medal or trophy, to not more than six state employes annually for outstanding service to the state.

52. Permit prunes of the 1964–65 crop grown north of the Tehachapi Mountains which remain unprocessed on May 1, 1965, to contain not more than two parts per million of chlorobenzilate for prunes processed into concentrate or juice.

53. Require higher fees for the issuance of permits to solicit or sell correspondence courses of study beyond high school level.

54. To permit county board of supervisors to authorize the sheriff to search for and rescue lost persons or those who are in danger within or near the county and authorize the payment of expenses for such duty as a proper county charge.

55. Require that defamatory campaign literature regarding a candidate bear the name of the person responsible for it.

56. Prohibit the sale, as well as the giving away of, live chicks, rabbits, ducklings or other fowl as a prize for, or inducement to enter, any game or other competition or as inducement to enter a place of business, as well as a place of amusement.

57. Provide that it is not unlawful for information about prevention of conception to be disseminated for the purposes of public health education by any person who is not commercially interested in the sale of any medicine or means which may be used for the prevention of conception.

58. Provide that the term "100 feet of polling place," as used in the prohibition of electioneering on election day within 100 feet of a polling place, shall be measured from the point on the property line closest to the entrance of the polling place.

59. Require that notice posted inviting sealed proposals or bids for doing of "such work" rather than for doing of "the works ordered."

60. Exempt from taxation for any purpose human whole blood, plasma, blood products, blood derivatives and any human body parts held in a bank for medical purposes.

61. Require meetings of the Mount San Jacinto Winter Park Authority to be open and public pursuant to the Ralph M. Brown Act.

62. Provide that a minor may not possess a concealable firearm unless he has written permission of his parent or guardian.

63. Change definition of "sawed-off shotgun" so as to include a rifle having a barrel of less than sixteen inches in length.

64. Require persons selling tickets for passage aboard any vessel to have written authorization.

65. Declare it to be a finding of the legislature that orderly use of broadcasting, telecasting and photographic equipment at proceedings of public administrative agencies serves the public policy of the state that citizens be informed concerning such proceedings; and authorize radio and television coverage of proceedings of all meetings and hearings, other than certain adjudicative proceedings, of all state, county and municipal administrative agencies required by law to be open to the public.

66. Increase the salary of the marshal in San Diego municipal court, and increase the number of sergeant marshals by two, deputy marshals by nine and deputy marshal-matron by two, in municipal courts of San Diego County.

67. Make it unlawful to sell or offer for sale any article represented as American Indian-made, unless the article was produced wholly by American Indian labor, and pro-

vide that "Indian" means a person who is enrolled or is a lineal descendant of one enrolled with the Bureau of Indian Affairs, an Indian tribe, band or pueblo.

68. Revise provision concerning community recreation programs conducted by governing body of public authorities to provide that no events except amateur athletic contests, demonstrations or exhibits and other educational, rather than educational and noncommercial events, where admission is charged may be held pursuant to the chapter dealing with recreation programs.

69. Require every person who purchases English walnuts or almonds for processing or resale from persons other than licensed dealers, brokers, commission merchants, agricultural cooperatives or wholesalers, instead of when purchased for coin or currency other than at retail, to keep records pertaining to such purchases.

70. Add school buses to those vehicles that may be stopped in front of a public or private driveway to load or unload passengers when authorized to do so by local ordinance.

71. Delete provisions generally authorizing addition of fruit, fruit juices, chocolate, chocolate syrup and other syrups to make mixed milk or cream drink, and provide standards for flavored milk and flavored dairy drink.

72. Permit seller to assort and allow an authorized quantity discount to consumer who purchases a case containing 2.4 gallons or more of wine consisting of containers of the same brand and size, where this quantity sale is a single transaction and is accomplished in a single delivery.

73. Revise curd sizes of cauliflower.

74. Raise salaries of officers and attaches of Eureka municipal court in Humboldt County, and create positions of deputy clerks I, II and III, rather than just "deputy clerks," with an increase in the total number of deputy clerks.

75. Prohibit real estate licensee from publishing any advertisement pertaining to an activity for which a real estate license is required which does not contain a designa-

tion disclosing that he is performing acts for which a real estate license is required.

76. Increase from seven to nine the membership of the Adult Authority, and declare the intent of the legislature that the Adult Authority should discharge its responsibilities without a further increase in membership.

77. Add to required courses of study for grades seven to twelve instruction in public speaking.

78. Permit the alcoholic beverage department to reject protests before a hearing, except protests made by a public agency, public official or governing body of a city or county, if the department determines that such protests are false, vexatious or without reasonable or probable cause, and provide that if the department rejects such a protest and issues a license, the department must hold a hearing to revoke the license, and provide that these provisions shall not be construed as prohibiting or restricting any right which an individual making a protest might have to judicial proceeding.

79. Permit each county central committee of the Democratic Party to establish dues not to exceed $24 per year for elected and alternate members of the committee. Provides also that each committee may remove such members for nonpayment of dues.

80. Increase from $500 to $1,500 the revolving fund which may be established by the board of law trustees from money in the law library fund, and increase from $15 to $50 the maximum amount which may be expended from the revolving fund for each lawful purpose.

81. Increase the salary of the Alpine County district attorney from $3,900 to $5,100 and that of the auditor from $2,600 to $3,500.

82. Increase the fee for an artist manager's license from $50 to $100 and the fee for each artist manager's branch office from $25 to $50.

83. Permit clerk to compare voter's signature on an identification envelope with that appearing on the voter's application for an absentee ballot, as well as that appearing

on the duplicate affidavit of registration as already required by law.

84. Add to the morality training law the requirement that teachers, in addition to providing other moral training, shall teach pupils about kindness toward domestic pets and the humane treatment of living creatures.

85. Exempt tools of trade and automobile of reasonable value needed to seek or maintain employment from consideration in determining eligibility for county indigent aid, and require board of supervisors to determine which tools of trade are necessary and the reasonable value of such automobile.

86. Authorize a peace officer to order a pedestrian off a bridge or overpass if the officer has reasonable cause to believe that such a person is on the bridge or overpass to throw substances at, or shoot at, vehicles or occupants.

20

★★★★★★★★★★★★★★★★★★★
★★★★★★★★★★★★★★★★★★★

"I POLLED TEN PEOPLE IN MIAMI ABOUT APPORTIONMENT. I FOUND TWO OF THEM FOR IT, ONE AGAINST IT, THREE WHO SAID THEY LIKED IT FRIED, AND FOUR WHO SAID THEY HAD NEVER TASTED IT."

—Steve Trumbull,
Miami Herald
reporter (ret.)

★★★★★★★★★★★★★★★★★★★
★★★★★★★★★★★★★★★★★★★

Universally in the throes of microphilia, the state legislature has almost universally neglected reapportionment.

Few issues have been more thrashed over in recent years.

Critics have settled on malapportionment as a prime cause of legislative backwardness.

The issue led to the Supreme Court's historic one-man-one-vote decision and of course precipitated the major congressional debate over Senator Everett Dirksen's proposal to override the court.

One value of the widespread and protracted discussion of legislative apportionment is that it has helped stimulate much of the general study of legislative behavior that is now under way. At the same time, many commentators have tended to exaggerate the importance of malapportionment as a cause of legislative backwardness. Hence the Supreme Court's decision has raised many inordinate hopes that the cure of malapportionment will automatically cure the state legislature's chronic malaise.

These hopes rest on the belief that malapportionment

has resulted in profound rural-urban conflict and stalemate in the legislature. This belief has been nourished by widely circulated statistics familiar to all. Malapportionment is the only legislative fault susceptible to pure arithmetical expression and undoubtedly this has lent the issue some additional appeal in our statistics-minded society.

Before court actions had forced some adjustments, it was calculated in the early 1960s that in Nevada 8 per cent of the population could elect a majority of the state senate. Some comparable percentages were 10.7 in California, 12 in Florida, 12.8 in Arizona, 14 in New Mexico, 14.2 in Maryland—on up the scale to 47 per cent in Vermont, 47.7 in Missouri and 47.8 in Oregon.

Oregon's most populous senate district contained 69,-634 people, its smallest 29,917. Second from the bottom of the list, in terms of arithmetic equity, stood California, with 6,038,771 people in its largest senate district and 14,294 in its smallest.

These indices of representation differ in the various lower legislative houses but nonetheless reflect a similar picture, one that has been drawn with many journalistic metaphors.

The statistics seem to document the belief that the state legislature is an arena for continuous battle between the country boys and the city boys, as Virginia journalists depict the factions in apportionment struggles; or of New York's upstate "appleknockers" versus the metropolitan machine politicians; or of Florida's "Pork Chop Gang" of piney woods senators versus slickers from Miami and Tampa. Similarly, a reader of such lore tends to think of Illinois as a case of Chicago against downstate, and of Missouri as a case of St. Louis against the lawmakers from the sticks.

Beyond question, the country boys have been in charge all over the country. And doubtless a rural-urban conflict shows up glaringly in some legislative votes. In truth, however, it has shown up regularly on only one well-defined rural-urban issue—reapportionment itself. On other salient political issues—from taxation to urban planning to pollution control—the picture of rural-urban conflict is largely myth, not entirely but mostly.

The myth rests largely on the assumption that a legislative majority coming from rural areas represents and fights primarily for rural interests. There is a companion assumption about legislators from the cities.

From these two assumptions springs the commonly held picture, as Professor Noel Perrin noted in the *Yale Review*, "of a league of backwoods legislators, solidly united against the cities, and regularly conspiring to block legislation that cities want to have passed. . . . The chief trouble with the picture," he added, "is that it is false. Or, say, 90 per cent false."

A variety of scholarly studies support Perrin. George D. Young studied the Missouri legislature and reported: "In the House, the difficulty of passing city legislation does not come from rural members but from members of the city's own delegation. . . . It is almost invariably true that if the city's delegation is united upon a measure, it will be accepted by the entire General Assembly."

Professor David Derge of Indiana University studied 14,052 roll calls in Illinois and said: "The city's bitterest opponents in the legislature are the political enemies from within its own walls, and those camped in the adjoining suburban areas."

Even in backwoodsy Alabama Dr. Murray Clark Havens of the University of Alabama found the rural-urban division indecisive, concluding: "In the case of rural splits, which were frequent, urban representatives, fairly well united themselves, found it relatively easy to employ the ancient political device of the balance of power."

Three political scientists—Howard D. Hamilton, Joseph E. Beardsley and Carleton C. Coats—studied the behavior of Indiana's malapportioned lawmakers: "Rural-urban, or metropolitan v. nonmetropolitan, conflict is *not* [their emphasis] a strong factor in the General Assembly," they said. "Metropolitan senators do not vote as a phalanx, they generally divide their votes in about the same manner as their colleagues, and the bogey of a metropolitan dictatorship in the legislature in the event of a fair reapportionment is a myth."

The unfortunate thing about the prevalence of the rural-urban myth is that it veils the deeper truth, that the legislature's dismaying performance is caused by its subservience to the true constituency. The predominance of rural representatives is merely historical happenstance; the commercial and corporate community is not so foolish that it has failed regularly to work through the regularly controlling majority, nor so foolish that it would fail to resist a loss of that fine relationship by reapportionment.

But, naturally, it works through the city boys too. In Florida, realty interests opposing urban renewal plans found their loudest voice one session in a lawmaker from Jacksonville, the state's second largest city. On the other hand, while one might expect to find a rural lawmaker protecting that great asset of the countryside, clear streams and bubbling water, one actually finds quite the opposite. Florida's manufacturing interests in piney woods Taylor County obtained legislation in 1947 allowing them to pollute the Fenholloway River with chemical wastes; in 1965 it was a rural legislator who introduced a special bill to allow still *additional* pollution of the now stinking Fenholloway. The measure passed but was vetoed. But the point is simply to illustrate how rural and urban legislators served neither rural nor urban interests but the interests of the true constituency.

As reporter Robert Sherrill wrote in *Harper's* last year about the Florida situation: "Pork Chopism, after all, is not rural in character, only rural in origin. The economic Establishment has used the Pork Chop bloc to oppose progress only because the bloc was already there and willing to be used. But Pork Chopism can continue even when the cities have the predominant vote in the legislature. Many think it will."

Malapportionment, as an issue, is older than the Republic. In the colonies it was common practice to award oversized representation to the tidewater area; the new western counties got the short end of the stick then. This too was the arrangement desired by the predominant constituency of the time. Slave-holding planters dominated the tidewater areas, and the small farmers, slaveless and not always couth, populated the upland.

This malapportionment was written into most of the early constitutions and resulted in a series of political struggles in the early nineteenth century. ". . . The contests over reapportionment took on a distinctly conservative-liberal character," noted Kelly and Harrison in *The American Constitution*. "In the Virginia convention of 1829–30 there occurred a notable instance of such a struggle, during which the conservative easterners succeeded in incorporating elaborate provisions in the new constitution for the continuation of their political control."

The conservative easterners, of course, viewed popular control of the legislature as a hazard to property rights. This was the attitude of the true constituency of the time. It has not changed substantially today. Malapportionment has simply been a circumstance that has simplified the true constituency's chore of running things.

It would hardly be possible to select a better state than Florida to illustrate the deeper character of the reapportionment struggle.

By any index of representation its apportionment was still among the nation's worst at the start of the 1960s. Some 12 per cent of the population could elect a majority of the senate and the same percentage could control a majority of the house.

Glittering, hustling Miami down in Dade County with 935,047 inhabitants had one senator.

So did Jefferson County, a backwoodsy patch of Georgia-border land that contained 9,543 inhabitants, a county seat called Monticello, and a florid, aging convivial banker named S. Dilworth Clarke, who happened to be the senator from Jefferson, the dean of the state senate and once the president of that august body.

In his twilight years old Dil Clarke usually slouched in phlegmatic silence at the senate desk, communicating only with his cuspidor, but he could kill legislation or pass it as easily as he could shuck a boiled peanut. All he had to do was get up and say, "This is a bad bill." Chances are a majority of the senate would agree.

To protect Clarke's Jefferson County fiefdom a number of reapportionment bills were sent down the drain. One proposed to expand his tiny district by adding Liberty County to it. Although Liberty County too was sparsely populated, Dil Clarke doomed that measure by rising in the senate, scratching his rumpled shirt front, peering out over his spectacles and making the most eloquent speech of his life, typically brief: "Give me Liberty," he said, "and you give me death."

The senate rulers were hardly disposed to kill off Dil Clarke. He was not merely their dean, he was the good old patriarch of the senate majority, helpful in more ways than one, as will be discussed later. He was very nearly the patron saint of the Pork Chop Gang.

Despite a state constitutional requirement, the Florida legislature had never been apportioned fairly. Malapportionment of the house was written right into the constitution —one representative for each county and no more than three for the largest five counties. The constitution thus provided for automatic adjustments to each new census without providing for any substantial change at all. Despite all this, reapportionment had never caused a great stir until 1955, a year when the legislature was supposed to redistribute seats in line with the latest census.

In 1955 LeRoy Collins became governor. Unlike prior governors, Collins made a great public issue of reapportionment. For six years, during one part term of two years and a full term of four, Collins fought for reapportionment in regular and special sessions that went on for hundreds of frustrating and futile days.

While one-man-one-vote representation was not even

possible under the state constitution, Collins was unable to persuade the legislature to do the best possible, nothing close to it. From time to time the house would issue forth a bill, but the senate would promptly kill it or emasculate it.

In the popular lore and voluminous newspaper coverage of the time the battle thus found its locus in the senate. There, session after session, year by year, reapportionment ran into adamant opposition of a group of twenty to twenty-two state senators, a commanding majority in a body of thirty-eight. In a moment of genius, *Tampa Tribune* editor James Clendinen dubbed this coalition the Pork Chop Gang. Almost instantly the phrase became part of the public vocabulary.

The senate majority members took pride in the appellation, though it was intended to carry some derisive freight. From time to time senate majority bloc members would wear crudely lettered PCG lapel badges at legislative socials. Perhaps inevitably, their ineffectual opposition in the senate came to be known as the Lamb Chop Gang. This label never seemed a source of much pride to anyone.

If nothing else, the descriptives simplified coverage of the reapportionment struggle. But there was another effect. The labeling veiled the real nature of both the reapportionment fight and the Pork Chop Gang; it somehow simplified further the rural-urban myth.

On the basis of this myth and on arithmetical theories about representation, LeRoy Collins battled the apportionment issue with great zeal and a total lack of success. Only toward the end of the six years, when the fight was all but done, did Collins say the one thing that was most true about it. "Powerful business interests," he finally concluded, "had thwarted the effort to obtain fair apportionment." Unfortunately, Collins did not cast the issue in these terms before the legislature. It would have lent considerable interest to the fight.

It was customary to speak of the Pork Chop Gang as a "rural" bloc. Yet its membership included senators from

Jacksonville and Pensacola. Moreover, the PCG frequently carried with it the votes of senators from other urban centers, at various times Tampa and St. Petersburg and Orlando and Miami, when it pushed through its great mass of "special interest" bills—most of which slide through nearly unanimously anyway.

The only militant and persistent opposition to the PCG was led, on the other hand, by hard-hitting Senator Verle A. Pope from small townish St. Augustine, and by gangling Senator Doyle Carleton, Jr., from Wauchula—a village in the heart of ranch country than which one can hardly get much more rural.

Though the reapportionment fight gave the senate majority its pungent nickname, the PCG was in fact no more than the coalition of senatorial leaders who had developed the most intimate relationship with the true constituency. To its services the entire structure of the senate was dedicated. This is not a point that would spring out of an analysis of roll calls; that would merely corroborate the point. The primary agency of action was the committee system. The Pork Chop Gang could hardly have worked it more brazenly.

One of its judiciary committees was known semiofficially as the Killer Committee. For a couple of sessions it was headed by a bald-headed, affable divorce lawyer, Senator Bart Knight from Florida's rustic Panhandle. Once reporters intercepted Knight in a corridor to ask when his committee would meet on several bills of interest. He replied: "I just had a meeting walking down the hall." He had a pocket full of proxy votes.

Since the Pork Choppers invariably elected the senate president, who appointed committees and assigned bills to them, they encountered little procedural difficulty in achieving their ends. When W. Turner Davis was senate president he once assigned a severance tax bill to several specific committees—then "to all other committees which now exist or which may be created in the future." Davis was capable of greater subtlety. He was not called the "Old Gray Fox" in tribute to his graying hair.

The Pork Chop committee system was fantastically efficient. In the 1959 session Knight's Killer Committee even killed eight bills which Knight himself had introduced—but which, for some reason or another, he did not want passed. Other committees routinely disposed of progressive legislation, proposals for central purchasing systems, a consumer commission to guard against unethical business practices, a plan to turn over abandoned bank deposits to the state, a proposal to regulate billboard advertising, an integrity-in-government bill. Predictably enough, when a bill on abandoned deposits was finally passed, it was so written that banks and other financial institutions could bleed such deposits to death for years before escheating them to the public treasury.

One reporter who watched the senate's operations sighed one day and concluded: "The Kremlin itself could not have selected a group of men more fundamentally opposed to democratic government." The assessment should not in any way be construed to mean that the PCG had any leftist tendencies. They were for the American enterprise system all the way.

No bill was likely to get past them if it seemed unfavorable to the banks, the private utilities, the small-loan companies, the timber industry, the mineral industry, the liquor industry, the truckers, the railroads. This was evident from the recorded action, of course.

An intricate web of transactions bound the Pork Choppers to the true constituency. No Florida reporter revealed this better than Martin O. Waldron, then with the *Tampa Tribune*. Waldron wrote a series of stories that should have won him a Pulitzer, an honor that finally came to him when he went to work for the *St. Petersburg Times* and exposed corruption in the state turnpike authority.

In 1959, however, when the Pork Chop Gang was at the peak of its power and notoriety, Waldron dug deep behind the public personalities.

There at the heart of things was old Dil Clarke, the wealthy banker from little Monticello. Clarke had cemented normally cordial relationships with his fellows by making personal loans, as Waldron said, to "legislators, acting governors, lobbyists and just plain people." For instance, Senator Charley Johns, an insurance man from Starke, once senate president and once acting governor, had borrowed some $71,181 in personal loans from Clarke over a twenty-year period. They seldom split on issues. Clarke as well not only got two small-loan company bills passed for lobbyist Raeburn C. Horne, mentioned earlier, but lent *him* $10,000. Horne, now dead, was a close friend of his fellow resident of Madison, Florida, W. Turner Davis, the former senate president who succeeded Horne as small-loan lobbyist. It was at Horne's fishing camp that the Pork Choppers frequently met.

Waldron also examined the fiscal background of the dark-haired, sharp-faced 1959 senate president, Dewey Johnson, a lawyer from Quincy, a listed attorney for the powerful St. Joe Paper Company, a Du Pont industry and owner of a huge chunk of West Florida timberlands; Johnson was also the borrower of large sums of money from the Du Pont chain of Florida national banks—all of which he explained, logically enough, as normal business borrowing secured by real estate. Johnson, like Turner Davis before him, slapped one modest severance tax bill into several committees including the Killer Committee—not long after he had served as director of a company that mined fuller's earth, and while he was still listed as attorney for it.

Among other Pork Choppers there was John Rawls, a hulking, moon-faced state senator who eventually became a circuit judge; while still a senator he was attorney for Florida Public Utilities Co. and West Florida Telephone Co. And there was, of course, Senator Wilson Carraway of Tallahassee, a banker and bottler who ruled the appropriations committee as chairman.

One of Waldron's most interesting revelations concerned a big, gruff, beetle-browed politician from Brooksville, James E. (Nick) Connor, who handled banking legislation directly until he succeeded to the senate presidency in the mid-1960s. Waldron recorded: "On March 27, 1959, a week before the opening of the last session of the Florida legislature, Sen. James E. (Nick) Connor borrowed $4,000 from the Hernando State Bank at Brooksville. Ten days later, on the second day of the session, Connor introduced a group of banking bills at the behest of bank lobbyist Alfred McKethan. The president of the bank where Connor borrowed the $4,000 happens to be McKethan. Connor, a land speculator, also borrowed $20,000 from McKethan's bank after the session closed. In both instances he put up land as collateral."

The tangle of business connections, similar ones and with some variations, went on and on. Out of it emerges a picture of a state senate leadership whose identity was inextricably merged with that of the true constituency. It may be that within the framework of the Pork Chop Gang there was more intraclique intercourse than in many states. It is highly doubtful, however, that its relationships with the commercial community were really extraordinary at all.

Certainly the real issue before the legislature during its interminable reapportionment squabble was not theoretical reapportionment. Nor was it merely the personal power of individual members. The great struggle was waged behind the apportionment issue: it was the struggle of the true constituency to prevent the dissolution of a perfect marriage.

By 1966, the pressure of court action had prompted the beginnings of reapportionment of the Florida legislature. The senate had been expanded. The Lamb Choppers had waged a successful fight to curb the rampant power of the Pork Chop Gang.

Nevertheless, the true constituency was not yet widowed. One recently published study by the Florida State University Institute of Governmental Research predicted that the reapportioned legislature will "reinforce rather than alter political, economic, and social patterns in the state."

To that, Bob Sherrill added: "The accuracy of this prediction is assured, first by the regularity with which even today Duval County (Jacksonville), second largest county in the state, sides with the small-county bloc against Dade (Miami); and, second, by the probability that, whatever apportionment plans Florida settles for over the next few years, the result will be a larger body. With that comes the kind of additional confusion in which the long-established power structure can continue to have its way. . . . That old gang of ours may become outnumbered, but confusion will still be riding on their side."

None of these comments are intended to disparage fair reapportionment as a desirable goal. One intent is merely to dampen what appear to be undue hopes raised by the prospect, thanks to the courts, of eventually attaining that goal. In the few recently reapportioned states some observers report at least evidence of new energy in the legislative halls.

Curiously, the most striking thing about the activity of the newly apportioned Michigan legislature, with the cities now amply represented, was its attention to a variety of farm legislation. The Michigan lawmakers, reapportioned and basking in unaccustomed praise (". . . more professional, better informed," said the *Detroit Free Press*), also promptly began pressing for a $5,000 yearly pay raise. During one session the salary boost passed the house; during another session it passed the senate. Then in 1966 the legislators decided to drop the whole idea, for the moment, in the face of a certain amount of fresh public disfavor—a result of the fact that several lawmakers wound up in trouble with the law. The federals charged one state senator with income tax delinquency, and the locals charged another with inviting a Michigan State University coed to go to bed with him and pose for some nude pictures; one freshman lawmaker was picked up on a drunk-driving charge and another house member found himself ticketed for careless driving following an accident—at about the same time a senator was fined for driving with an expired license; meanwhile, the state senator already hooked for tax delinquency also spent a night in jail after being picked up for drunk driving. Michigan wits offered the legislature a wry defense

("It's unfair," said one, "to blame the entire legislature for the mistakes of half its members"), while one state official suggested that the session should be summarized under two categories: "Acts passed" and "Acts committed." In any event, the pay-raise idea cooled off. So did the unaccustomed praise.

In Colorado, House Speaker Allan Dines cited a number of actions taken by his newly reapportioned legislature, not all of them spectacularly impressive. He singled out the legislative attention to local government, saying: "No less than 29 bills were passed in the area of local governmental affairs, ranging from a local dog leash law to a new statute on municipal annexation. The latter, a compromise between urban and suburban viewpoints, was of particular significance. It broke a long deadlock created by the vetoes of two prior annexation bills—bills on which *urban and rural legislators had in the past combined* to treat suburban interests a bit harshly." (Emphasis mine.) Speaker Dines mentioned other legislation, then went on to say:

"Reapportionment was not, in and of itself, responsible for all of this legislation. But to a significant extent, I think, it contributed to all by creating what one might call an atmosphere for action, not inaction, and by breaking up some long-standing, internal legislative alliances which had tended toward inaction. I confess that the 1965 Colorado General Assembly fought long and hard—within itself and with the governor—over taxing and spending. *With or without reapportionment, however, this battle would have occurred in much the same fashion,* for it was a partisan and a philosophical battle as these annual disagreements over budgets invariably are." (My emphasis.)

My guess is that with but minor differences, if any, state legislative behavior in all fields will follow much the same fashion with reapportionment as without. Historic and chronic malapportionment simply has not been a root cause of the legislative malaise. It has been but the most brazen of the symptoms of the state legislature's alienation from the people. It has seemed the most brazen only because it has been the most easily measured, and has been such an indisputable default of duty, not subject to debate except among political sophists, an unanswerable affront to the democratic idea.

21

(decorative star border)

"IT IS TOO EARLY FOR POLITICIANS TO PRESUME ON OUR FORGETTING THAT THE PUBLIC GOOD, THE REAL WELFARE OF THE GREAT BODY OF THE PEOPLE, IS THE SUPREME OBJECT TO BE PURSUED; AND THAT NO FORM OF GOVERNMENT WHATEVER HAS ANY OTHER VALUE THAN AS IT MAY BE FITTED FOR THE ATTAINMENT OF THIS OBJECT. WERE THE PLAN OF THE CONVENTION ADVERSE TO THE PUBLIC HAPPINESS, MY VOICE WOULD BE, REJECT THE PLAN. WERE THE UNION ITSELF INCONSISTENT WITH THE PUBLIC HAPPINESS, IT WOULD BE ABOLISH THE UNION. IN LIKE MANNER, AS FAR AS THE SOVEREIGNTY OF THE STATES CANNOT BE RECONCILED TO THE HAPPINESS OF THE PEOPLE, THE VOICE OF EVERY GOOD CITIZEN MUST BE, LET THE FORMER BE SACRIFICED TO THE LATTER. HOW FAR THE SACRIFICE IS NECESSARY HAS BEEN SHOWN. HOW FAR THE UNSACRIFICED RESIDUE WILL BE ENDANGERED IS THE QUESTION BEFORE US."

—*The Federalist Papers*
(No. 45: Madison)

21

To speak of the alienation of the state legislature is not to assert that it *never* dips into the main currents of American thought and development. To speak of the state's irrelevancy to the development of the national society is not to declare that it has no meaning whatever.

To emphasize these relative qualities, as I have, is merely to insist that the state—the state legislature—has provided little of the impetus, the force, the energy, the creativity in the fashioning of the society.

With their various reasons to insist that the states are strong and vital, politicians will continue to cite the enormous sums that represent cumulative state spending. Like the distances of astronomy, these figures tend to impress. Yet they stand as a testament to the strength and vitality of the states no more than Tommy Manville's annual budget attests to his own strength of character. Manville doubtless has had motives for increased spending, but it has not necessarily meant that he had become a better man.

As for the cumulative budget of the states, the impetus for its growth has come primarily from the programming in Washington. Statistics suggesting fantastically blossoming state vitality are familiar to all. By 1962, the year of the latest comprehensively accurate figures, it was possible to show that state *and local* government spending nearly quintupled between 1946 and 1962, increasing from $14.1 billion to $70.1 billion. By contrast, federal spending in that period grew only 62.5 per cent—from $66.5 billion to $106.4 billion. With such figures as these, some observers suggest a new era of state vitality. Yet, even excluding the fact that most of the state-local total is purely local, relying on no state initiative at all, the figures mislead further. For one thing, much of the state programming has been stimulated only by the federal government; grants-in-aid increased from 5.3 per cent of state-local revenue in 1946 to 11.3 per cent in 1962—and of the sixty U.S. grant-in-aid programs that existed in the latter year, Congress enacted thirty-even of them after World War II, a crucial fact that led the authoritative *Congressional Quarterly* to observe: "By limiting comparisons to the postwar period . . . one obtains a distorted picture of the relative fiscal growth of federal, state and local governments. At the beginning of this period the Federal Government had just experienced extraordinary wartime expansion, and the state and local governments had postponed all but unavoidable expenditures for the duration of the war. If one uses as a base year fiscal 1938, when state and local expenditures ($10.0 billion) exceeded those of the Federal Government ($8.4 billion), a radically different picture of relative growth emerges." In other words, in the recent upsurge of spending, the states haven't been gaining on the problems at hand but, mostly, just catching up on historic neglect. The truth is that until the expanded federal program of the 1950s, the states were sloughing off even their commonest function: road building. No one who has studied the legislature supposes that the states, without the nudging of federal ideas and the inducement of matching money, would have contributed much to the system of welfare and health programs that are gradually improving the lot of the whole people of this country.

That simple notion I take to be both the purpose and the impulse of American society: to improve the lot of the whole people. The American social revolution has been only the doing of it, the alternate inching and leaping forward. It has been a revolution that has been so slow, so controlled that it would not even be called a revolution were there not a history of nearly two centuries of sporadic violence to remind us that it is.

The explosion of black frustration in Watts is not an immeasurable distance from the explosion caused by the tatterdemalion would-be combatants who followed the luckless Daniel Shays in Massachusetts—albeit the armed farmers who patrolled the roads of the corn country in the 1930s were closer kin to Shays: they too were beset by creditors and deprived of relief by state government adamant or impotent or both. It was a fresh awareness and wariness of Shays—that "desperate debtor" as he is called in the *Federalist*—that impelled the Founding Fathers to beget the nation; it was a poignant consciousness of the smouldering plight of the farmer in the Great Depression that put wind in the sails of New Deal relief legislation. As well, it was a stark recognition that Watts could happen again and again that, just yesterday, made the nation wonder whether the war on poverty was not more than mere political charity. Violence sparks every revolution—even a slow and generally peaceful one.

Here I begin to conclude these notes and comments. I shall do with some ruminations about the country's history. My purposes are to suggest that there is no cause for astonishment at the condition and character of the state legislature today, simply because their peculiar institutional mentality and mores come to them by legacy; and to suggest that the alienation and irrelevancy of the state legislature is a natural, perhaps an inevitable condition, simply because the state—the legislature—fell inexorably into the role of an antirevolutionary institution in a society whose sometimes slow but persisting impulse is revolutionary. Counterrevolution becomes passé as a revolution nears completion.

I do not speak here of the political revolution that transferred the seat of political power from England to America. Rather, I speak of the social revolution, which had hardly begun in 1776 and which continues today, the revolution through which the frecklebellies and peckerwoods have gradually obtained some sharing of the goodies of the earth.

Turn where you will in the American past and you find most often the state resisting that revolution, blocking or countering or delaying the efforts of the common man to take hold of his fate. Some historians like to think of the Constitution as a counterrevolutionary document, hence of Washington and the federal government as a creature of counterrevolution. Still, with whatever delay, it has been the national government through which America's lesser folk have finally attained a voice, some voice in society's decisions.

Most often the state has played another role, not always as blatantly as Arizona, whose government in 1917 literally loaded some 1,000 striking copper-mine workers onto boxcars and hauled them out of the state, dumping them in New Mexico. Not always that blatantly but frequently as pointedly as West Virginia. After World War I, West Virginia's legislature was aiming squarely at radical labor leaders when it made it unlawful to teach "ideals hostile to those now or henceforth existing under the constitution and laws of the state."

In that same post-World War I era at least twenty-four states passed "syndicalism" or "anarchy" laws aimed primarily at labor organizers. Under the wispy umbrella of a California statute (to outlaw doctrine suggesting the use of force to bring about a change in industrial ownership) more than five hundred persons were arrested in five years.

Here, then, in these instances, was the natural institutional reflex of the state legislature. As the laboring man moved to obtain a decision-making voice in industry, the legislature celebrated the menaced commercial orthodoxy—with a vengeance. Several legislatures, with no greater permanent success, had already prohibited the teaching of evolution. In the light of it all no one should be surprised at the instances of antidemocratic, antiliberty, anti-intellectual sentiment that recur so frequently in the state legislature of today—no one who has read history with a cool eye. Only in April 1966 did the U.S. Supreme Court throw out an Arizona loyalty oath law that, though written in 1961, might have been drafted a generation or so earlier by the same politicians who ordered the union organizers bundled onto trains and hauled out of the state.

Too often we in America read our history with a warm and misting eye. We read it to extract doctrine, to multiply our slogans. If this is inevitable and necessary (it is both; it provides the emotional glue that sticks us together), it is also distracting. We tend to remember the rhapsodic phrases and pungent place-names that evoke heroic epochs with bite-sized words. We tend to forget salient particulars.

We tend to remember Massachusetts as the citadel of antislavery principle and to forget that it was not an act of the state of Massachusetts that freed the slaves early. It was the act of a slave named Quock Walker. He sued his master for his freedom—on the ground that the state constitution's slogan, "All men are born free and equal," meant what it said—and he won.

We tend to remember the quest for religious liberty that helped people the colonies, and to forget that as late as 1817 in New Hampshire, 1818 in Connecticut and 1833 in Massachusetts the state government required the payment of religious taxes, and that it took Jefferson, Madison and R.H. Lee seven years to get the Virginia legislature to adopt the Statute of Religious Liberty. Patrick Henry supported a counterplan to support all churches by taxation.

It is more uplifting to remember Henry's inspirationals in behalf of liberty than to recall his pathetic inability to act on what his conscience told him about slavery: "Would anyone believe," he wrote a friend, "that I am Master of Slaves of my own purchase! I am drawn along by the general inconvenience of living without them; I will not, I cannot justify it. However culpable my conduct . . . I believe a time will come when an opportunity will be offered to abolish this lamentable evil."

Patrick Henry was the prisoner of a status quo that was generous indeed to him, and the state was not designed as an instrument for undoing it. Liberty, to him, was the severance of Virginia's political ties to England. Henry was no mouthpiece for the common man; he was not *that* revolutionary.

And here was the common attitude among the comparatively few men who ran things. To perceive this is to understand how they might have stood—did stand—as true Jacobins until free of England, then how they turned the state into a damper of the more general popular impulses to freedom and equality.

Consider Sam Adams and Massachusetts—first Sam Adams as a flaming revolutionary and Massachusetts as a colony, then Sam Adams as an elder statesman and Massachusetts as a state.

There was no more authentic American Jacobin than Adams. It was he who inflated the shooting of four or five Bostonians into an inflammatory "massacre." After the East India Company obtained a tea monopoly and threatened to undersell American merchants, it was Adams who managed the Boston Tea Party. Came the countermeasures from Parliament: the closing of the Boston port. The people of Massachusetts found themselves economically beleaguered but unable to obtain relief through political avenues. They protested, agitated and began to lay up arms and supplies.

It was to destroy such stores that General Thomas Gage, the crown's governor, sent an armed expedition to Lexington and Concord in 1775. Gage was routed and all but besieged at Boston. Even before the Battle of Bunker Hill, however, Gage issued a proclamation pardoning many of the American insurrectionaries. But not Sam Adams. Gage said Adams' offenses were "of too flagitious a nature to admit of any other consideration than that of condign punishment." He thought Adams should be put to death.

This schoolboy history is put down only as a refresher and background against which to observe what happened a short time later in the new *state* of Massachusetts. The war was over. Hard times came, partly the result of the precipitate depreciation of paper money at the end of hostilities, partly because accustomed markets were shut off. The state began to press for overdue taxes. Merchants pressed to collect due debts. An inundation of court orders fell against thousands of small farmers who had come out of the army and gone into debt for supplies and gear. Pressures on them to pay increased just as their chances of selling produce decreased. Bad everywhere, the situation was worse in Massachusetts. Some state governments tried to alleviate conditions. Not Massachusetts. Commercial interests that had framed the state constitution also controlled the General Court. Relief was not forthcoming. Courts were jammed up with suits for debts. And the farmers found that lawyers did not offer their services as a form of charity.

Thus the farmers were economically beleaguered but unable to obtain relief through political avenues. They protested, they agitated, they began to lay up arms and supplies. More or less accidentally, an ex-Army captain named Daniel Shays assumed the leadership. In 1786 he and his followers hoped to exert enough power to prevent further judgments for debt until a state election could be held. To disperse and dispel them the governor dispatched the militia into the field—a military action kindred in spirit to that commanded by General Gage little more than a decade earlier. Though most of the rebels were spared and Shays escaped, we discover Samuel Adams now expressing a sentiment common in the Massachusetts legislature. The rebels were "wicked and unprincipled men." Adams thought Shays should be put to death.

Shays' Rebellion, in the run-of-the-survey history book, is often a springboard for a discussion of monetary and currency problems in the newly independent colonies. It is cited as an episode that impelled the leaders of the day to make haste in putting together a union government with general monetary powers. It is well documented that the rebellion frightened the monied classes of the day. It starkly dramatized the antagonism between the populous poor and the controlling rich; between the debtor class and the propertied class. At the time it was still thought that relief could be granted the former only at the expense of the latter; the rise of the poor would mean the fall of the rich. It has taken the country a long time to discover that this is not so.

In any event, I mention the episode of Shays' Rebellion for no such harangue on economics. I recount it only to illustrate how in this situation the state fell naturally into the position of opposing Shays' quest for an economic break, which was all that was sought—as one 1786 petition from a group of debtors to the Massachusetts government shows:

> We beg leave to inform your honours that unless something takes place more favourable to the people, in a little time att least one half of our inhabitants in our oppinion will become banckerupt. . . . Sutes att law are very numerous and the atturneys in our oppinion very extravagant and oppressive in their demands. And when we compute the taxes laid upon us the five preceding years: the state and county, town and class taxes, the amount is equil to what our farms will rent for. Sirs, in this situation what have we to live on—no money to be had; our estates dayly posted and sold, as above described. . . . Suerly your honours are not strangers to the distresses of the people but doe know that many of our good inhabitants are now confined in gole for det and for taxes; many have fled, others wishing to flee to the State of New York or some other State.

Later, when Shays and his followers took up arms, it must be argued, the state had no choice but to put them down. It had to insure order and tranquility. To be sure. Yet, there had been an alternative. It had already been by-passed, the alternative of providing relief before men were driven to arms.

The state government's simple choice was either to answer the wants of the people or to move against them when their needs drove them to militancy. It is a choice that state government has confronted countless times. Habitually if not invariably state government has elected to follow a course like that charted in Massachusetts in 1786. That is, its tendency has been not to assist the lesser man's drive for improvement but to resist it.

Repeatedly the common man's thwarted aspirations

have been kindled into violence, and invariably at that point
—its true alternative by then vanished—state government
has fulfilled its indisputably proper function of suppressing
the threats to order and tranquility. Thus state government
has always managed to dramatize its antirevolutionary
stance in the pious name of law and order.

Actually, of course, in this repeatedly recurring sequence, the state government has inevitably reflected and
executed the will of the true constituency to preserve the
existing social and economic order. The mere fact that this
stance has been inevitable, however, would scarcely dimin-
ish its effect on the conscious and submerged attitudes of
the mass of lesser people whose lot has been improved in
the social revolution. Upon this inexact and subtly woven
texture of the people's national memory state government
has impinged itself as a force that is habitually hostile to the
advancement of the lesser people.

Thus in this era, particularly the last three decades,
when the quest for democracy and economic equity has
achieved handsome gains through federal channels, it is not
in the least surprising that state government, particularly
the policy-making legislature, has about it those qualities of
irrelevancy and alienation. It would be difficult—and preposterous—for any working American who has at length
attained any voice in shaping his small fraction of the economy to identify at all with the state government. Its history
of hostility to the change that social improvement entails
has been too persistent and too often dramatized in a way
that can be understood even by the unlettered.

In this time of the Negro revolution many instances
will come to mind illustrating this habitual stance of state
government. The sequence is always the same. State government resists the quest for betterment until the thwarted
aspirations are kindled into hazardous demonstrations or
outright violence, and then the authority and forces of the
state are pitted against the aspirants in the name of law and
order. This has been most visible in the southern states only
because the dramatizations of it have been frequent and

starkly defined. Nonetheless the Negro revolution is a national development, and throughout the nonsouthern part of the country, from New York to California, outbreaks of racial violence have been frequent—and state government has been far more visible in enforcing peace and order than in helping the Negro improve his lot.

Many students of the American system commonly suggest that the people have turned to Washington because state government has "not been responsive" to their needs. This, I suggest, is euphemism. At the crucial turning points of the social revolution state government has assumed a posture of outright hostility to the advancement of the lesser people.

Some dramatizations of this have been more vivid than others. Many of the most vivid occurred in the early years of the Great Depression, a generation before Orval Faubus posted his National Guard at the door of Central High School in Little Rock (to preserve law and order and incidentally keep out several Negro pupils) but about 150 years after the Massachusetts government routed Shays' desperate debtors (to preserve order and the hard money of the creditor class). In the surge of labor activity in the early Depression state government repeatedly showed itself in the stance of the protector of the corporate constituency against the worker. It took action not to assist the worker's quest for a voice in his economic life but, in the name of law and order, commonly put the forces of the state at the disposal of the challenged industrial order.

In 1934, when a United Textile Workers strike spread up and down the Eastern Seaboard Georgia's Governor Gene Talmadge threw pickets into a concentration camp, and the governor of North Carolina ordered out his state guard at the request of the textile companies. "In nearly every instance," old Tarheel Josephus Daniels wrote, "the troops might as well have been under the direction of the mill owners." Up in Rhode Island the troops were called into action too, and the trade journal *Fibre and Fabric* left no doubt about the attitude of the textile industry: "A few hundred funerals," it said, "will have a quieting influence." To illustrate points about the "travail of labor" Schlesinger recounts these episodes in *The Coming of the New Deal*.

I mention them with two points in mind. One is that it is in this stance as the resistant of social change that state government has most emphatically impressed itself upon the deeper American folk memory, hence it has naturally come to seem almost a futile eddy in the main current of American development. The second point is simply that in the nature of things this has been more or less inevitable. Granted the stubborn resistance to change that sets the stage for desperate action, state government is impelled into its accustomed stance simply by virtue of its basic role as a police power. In Minneapolis in 1934 a truckers' strike took on most of the aspects of open revolution, reaching a nightmarish climax when police fired shotguns into a crowd that gathered where unarmed pickets had tried to block a strike-breaking vehicle; the blasts killed two and wounded sixty-seven (and eyewitness reporter Eric Sevareid wrote: "Suddenly I knew, I understood deep in my bones and blood what Fascism was"). Minnesota's governor at the time, Floyd Olson, ultimately arrested the strike leaders. Recounting this event, Schlesinger notes: "Floyd Olson considered himself a radical and a friend of the workers. But he was also governor of the state of Minnesota and determined to uphold the public authority." In short, he had no choice. It is equally true that he had had little success in persuading the Minnesota legislature to adopt progressive ideas that would have helped prepare the way for social change on various fronts—the alternative that seems so seldom to have been exercised by state government. What might have been obtained by law *with* order was left to vagrant events. Schlesinger summed up the consequences in Minneapolis: "After a civil conflict stretching over four months, wide loss in property and wages, violence, death and martial law, the employers of Minneapolis conceded the right of the truckers to be represented by their own union."

Perhaps no era is better than the Great Depression for the student of state government's reflexes. Here was the time when no man with sight could fail to see the urgent need for action, innovation, social and economic change. The aura of revolution flared visibly, and revolution was freely predicted. By 1934 the mayor of one Massachusetts town, urging expanded federal job programs, wrote: "If some such remedial measure is not immediately adopted I make bold to predict fundamental and sweeping changes in the structure of our government before the end of the present year."

Between 1927 and 1932 at least 10 per cent of the nation's farm property had been foreclosed. "In certain sections of the West," as Commager and Steele recorded, "these foreclosures had become so numerous that farmers banded together to intimidate prospective purchasers, close courts, and terrorize judges, recalling the scenes of Shays' Rebellion a century and a half earlier." From the states they got no relief. The fires were put out only by U.S. action providing farm mortgage relief.

What had state government been up to? How did it react? After FDR was in office Harry Hopkins, responding to Alf Landon's insistence that relief should be a local responsibility, snorted that "The Governor of Kansas has never put up a thin dime for the unemployed in Kansas." Actually, as others pointed out, although Kansas had contributed nothing for relief, it did put up some $200,000 to help administer the program. Here was a state that in the previous century had managed to contribute some $75 million to subsidize the railroads.

As the Depression began there were no state laws that effectively protected wages. In 1932 Philip F. LaFollette coaxed and prodded the Wisconsin legislature to adopt the country's first unemployment compensation plan. Almost invariably, state politicians cite this as a prime instance of the imagination and vitality and creativity of the state legislature.

The fact is that nearly every European state had pioneered unemployment plans in the prior generation.

Few states had developed any plans to protect the aged. Eight legislatures in the 1920s enacted optional old-age pension laws. And in 1933 ten states approved mandatory acts. Still, roughly half the states had no old-age laws at all. When the situation did prompt energetic state government action, the legislative mind appeared to be on other things.

In a single year, June 1934 to June 1935, fully forty-four states considered sedition and teachers' oath legislation, and in those twelve months the American Civil Liberties Union "recorded a greater variety and number of serious violations of civil liberties than any year since the war."

The states, in short, hoped to stamp out the revolutionary fires and rout the revolutionaries, who included, according to the creative Wisconsin legislature, faculty members at the University of Wisconsin—"an ultra liberal institution in which communistic teachings were encouraged and where avowed communists were welcome." Among others, the Illinois legislature also busied itself more hunting witches in schools than in improving the conditions of the unemployed; after all, drugstore magnate Charles R. Walgreen had withdrawn a niece from the University of Chicago because she had been exposed there to Red propaganda and free love.

This legislative clamor, of course, reflected the anxieties of the true constituency, whose sufferings were sometimes heart-rending. "Five Negroes on my place in South Carolina," complained Du Pont vice president Robert R. M. Carpenter in 1934, "refused work this spring, after I had taken care of them and given them house rent free and work for three years during bad times, saying they had easy jobs with the government. . . . A cook on my houseboat at Fort Myer quit because the Government was paying him a dollar an hour as a painter."

The anguish and fears of the true constituency found their natural voice in the state legislature and, elsewhere, in the Liberty League, whose members, as William E. Borah dryly pointed out, ". . . were deeply moved about the Constitution of the United States. They had just discovered it."

The unattractive general truth is that throughout the Depression era, when the present American system began to take shape, state government generally responded to the people's need for bread by providing them circuses featuring witch hunts in one ring and barkers spouting the old laissez-faire notions of liberty in the other. FDR sometimes put the matter in wry perspective: "I am not for a return to that definition of liberty," he said, "under which for many years a free people were being gradually regimented into the service of the privileged few." Pennsylvania Governor George H. Earle saw through it all, too, declaring that communism was not so great a danger as allowing "our men of wealth to send us on a wildgoose chase after so-called radicals while they continue to plunder the people."

When Herbert Hoover wrote a book defending the businessman's notions of individual liberty and asked Harlan F. Stone to comment on it, Justice Stone came right to the point: "Even the man in the street," he said, "is aware that every important reform in the past seventy-five years has been resisted and assailed as an infringement of individual liberty."

Such, generally, was the reflex of state government in those dark times. Facing crying needs for change, they resisted and assailed and celebrated the passing orthodoxy. The period left few sentimental illusions about the states intact. When the New Deal was discussing the possibility of proposing a constitutional amendment to overcome court resistance to minimum-wage legislation, FDR himself assayed the chances an amendment would face among state legislatures. Schlesinger quoted him in *Politics of Upheaval.* "To get a two-thirds vote, this year or next year, on any type of amendment is next to impossible. . . . You could make five million dollars as easy as rolling off a log by undertaking a campaign to prevent ratification by one house of the legislature, or even the summoning of a constitutional convention,

in thirteen states for the next four years. Easy money. . . .
If I were John W. Davis and had five hundred thousand
dollars, I could stop a constitutional amendment cold."

In this private comment to a correspondent, Roosevelt
detailed the amount it would take to fix each of thirteen
states. The 1930s, after all, were the period during which,
according to Harold Zink's *Government and Politics in the
United States*, "The Indiana General Assembly . . . had
enough grafters among its members that a regular scale
of prices was drafted for quotation to those who sought
improper favors."

The reaction of state government to the Depression was
traditional and customary, not unusual.

As America became a nation political control was
tightly held by an elite of professional and commercial
men who regarded liberty as important only so long as it
helped the acquisition of private property. Conversely, the
advocacy of individual rights was often held to be a menace
to property rights. These attitudes were hardly secret.

In 1821 when a New York convention was revising the
state constitution this outlook was tersely expressed by
James Kent, a state legislator, law professor and supreme
court judge. "The tendency of universal suffrage," he said,
"is to jeopardize the rights of property, and the principles
of liberty. . . . The individual who contributes only one cent
to the common stock, ought not to have the same power and
influence in directing the property concerns of the partnership, as he who contributes his thousands."

Property and religious restrictions abounded at the
time the Constitution was adopted. Artisans and working
people had no say in the government for the most part. Less
than three per cent of the white male population partici-
pated in the elections that ratified the U.S. Constitution,
and state government was not notably fast in advancing
notions of democracy.

Instead, in most instances, the state legislature
promptly set to work establishing systems of apportionment

that tended to leave power in hands that held it despite population growth and westward migration—the practice only recently ruled illegal by the U.S. Supreme Court. Rule by oligarchy was the usual situation. "Until the 1820s less than 5 per cent of the people customarily voted even in important elections," it was noted in *The American Constitution*. From the beginning state government tended to resist the impulses for social change. Only when these impulses became menacingly strong did response tend to be forthcoming—and then too little. State government represented essentially the same establishment after the war as before. The primary traditions that played upon them were commercial and ecclesiastical, not political. The line of tradition behind the Virginia legislature leads back not to the English parliamentary system but to a commercial corporate structure pioneered by the great Italian merchants after the mercantile idea came to propel European states at the passing of the Middle Ages. The mercantile mentality of the Virginia legislature is as evident today as ever. Its institutional ancestor was the joint stock company—the Virginia Company of London.

This company was run by a governor and council appointed in London. All this is familiar, of course, but too often forgotten when observers of today are trying to assess the legislature. These corporate officers presided over the Jamestown fiasco and other commercial disasters that tended to demoralize the participants. To buck things up and encourage further immigration the company's London proprietors in 1618 attempted a reorganization in which the governor was to set up a local representative assembly —a body patterned on the company's "general court" or stockholders' meeting in London. This was the beginning of the Virginia colonial legislature. It has run the state like a company property ever since. Also, just as in the parent company in London, there was an advisory "council" that used to sit with the assembly when it met. After further financial failure, the king finally yanked the company's charter and turned Virginia into a royal domain. ". . . But the frame of government of the Old Dominion, both as colony and as state, continued to be that imposed by the joint-stock company." That's the way *The American Constitution* put it.

These historical giblets may be useful. There is a persistent tendency among Americans, including many legislators, to think that our state governmental forms are somehow patterned on the English parliamentary system, despite the fact that when our colonies were being put together the Parliament had not taken on its familiar shape yet.

We further tend to discover all manner of weighty doctrine to explain why there are two houses in nearly all American legislatures. The historic reasons were not complex at all. The "councils" stopped sitting with the "assemblies" for essentially the same reasons that vice presidents who are on General Motors' executive committee do not use the same men's room as lesser executives. They are richer and feel more important and tend to develop facilities and practices which set them off. The truth is that they think they smell better. Such corporate status symbols have been widely publicized lately. It was no different in the seventeenth century. "American bicameralism was . . . largely an outgrowth of colonial social and economic distinctions, with the council and assembly drawing apart because they represented different economic interests." I got that from *The American Constitution* too. It offers one of the most lucid analyses of the origins of the American forms ever written.

As a matter of practice, the councils, appointed by the crown or proprietor on the governor's recommendation, were usually drawn from the landed gentry and merchant class. This meant that they had been sufficiently instructed so that they seldom caught the flesh of a matron's belly when they snapped their snuff boxes shut. On the other hand the smaller fish who constituted the assemblies could not be regarded as so reliable. The others wanted to keep them at a distance. So they sat apart from them. Presto: two houses.

Doctrines lauding these "checks and balances" within the legislature were invented later to justify, explain and defend conditions that, although they did not appear quite rational, sprang out of these quite common facts of life.

These matters are important not merely as historical curiosities. Out of these events developed the great body of custom and tradition that plays upon the state legislature today. The force of custom and tradition invariably outweighs the force of theory.

Not all the colonial governments sprang directly from a joint stock company apparatus, but the joint stock forms tended to be widely copied. The Plymouth Colony, of course, was established by the Puritans—so called because they wanted to purify, not themselves, but the English church of popery. The compact that they put together on the Mayflower represented an adaptation of John Calvin's theory of how a church is formed—that is, by "common consent" of the members. For reasons that baffle me historians always cheer this notion as the very foundation stone of the idea of "consent of the governed." Actually, this notion lies back there somewhere when the first male (or female) planted a stone axe into the head of somebody who told him to do some disagreeable chore. No matter.

The Mayflower compact, anyway, governed the Plymouth Colony for its entire existence. It lasted seventy-one years. Some other colonial covenants similarly had an ecclesiastical origin but nevertheless tended to adapt to the company-state methods being used around them. Most historians regard the Fundamental Orders of Connecticut (1639) as the first written constitution of this country.

It created a government patterned directly on that found in the joint-stock company organization of Massachusetts Bay. In Massachusetts the "General Court" was the quarterly stockholders' meeting. It became the legislature. According to Connecticut's Fundamental Orders the colonial freeman assembled yearly in a "courte of election" and elected deputies to sit in a General Court.

The most noticeable importation of English political

methods could be observed in those colonies that were established as feudal grants—New York, Maryland, New Jersey, Pennsylvania, Delaware, the Carolinas and Georgia. Schemes to set up feudal governments were common but did not work simply because land was too plentiful in America to sustain a system based on land scarcity. It makes you cringe to think what the founding fathers would have founded if land had been scarce.

The colonial governments remained—while the original reasons for their existence gradually petered out. The joint-stock companies never fulfilled their owners' hopes of making great fortunes. The feudal enterprises proved such flops that the crown stopped setting them in motion after the Georgia venture. The puritan drive too had turned in different directions. Notions of religious liberty sputtered here and there, but most of Americans turned their attentions to their own forms of religious intolerance. A person could not vote in Massachusetts unless he was a Congregationalist. The Virginia assembly disfranchised non-Protestants after 1699. Catholics were disfranchised in Maryland, New York, Rhode Island, South Carolina and Virginia in the later colonial period.

This backward glance, of course, is not being conducted to bewail long-departed conditions but to discover the nativity of customs that shaped the American legislature. A citizen of 1966 is entitled, of course, to wonder whether there is any current validity in the attitudes that developed so long ago. For those who wonder, it is worth pointing out that one of the commonest, most universal traits of the state legislature—its hostility to the governor —has its emotional origins in this colonial period.

The legislature did in fact represent the attitudes of the top mercantile and commercial interests of the colonies. But the governor of a colony was still an appointee of the crown, usually actually selected by the English Board of Trade but appointed by the king. (Only Rhode Island and Connecticut chose their own governors in this period.) Thus the legislature came to look upon the governors as intruders.

The governors represented crown policies that increasingly conflicted with the intentions of the local entrepreneurs, the colonists. As a minion of the king the governor assumed and asserted the right to run everything. Inevitably the legislatures tended to fight against the governors for both emotional and practical reasons. Thus in 1721 the Massachusetts General Court informed Governor Shute that he would not be getting his annual salary until he had penned all the legislation enacted by the assembly. From time to time this gambit was recorded in New York, New Jersey, Pennsylvania. Such were examples of the hostility that developed between the legislature and the governor. The reasons for it are quite clear.

It is equally clear that *no* such reasons exist today. Yet hostility is everywhere observable between the state legislature and the governor. Though each governor is elected by all the people of the state, he is still regarded by the legislature with the suspicions and resistance with which the colonial legislators regarded the appointees of the crown. The fact of this attitude is among the reasons that the people of the states can elect one reform governor after another and find that his programs are seldom enacted into law.

Common sense suggests that when the people of a state voting as a whole have approved a program advocated by a candidate for governor, then the legislature should not have any great fear of enacting it into law. Yet the history of state politics in America is a story of reform programs crashing into smithereens on the rocks of legislative resistance. There are various reasons for this, but an important, unchanging justification for it all is the existence of a legislative hostility that some observers find incomprehensible. It is not incomprehensible at all to one who recognizes the overwhelming force of custom. Custom has a staying power that quite defies reasonable explanation. (When the Pope visited New York in 1965 many people inquired why he wears a skull cap. One television commentator cleared up the question. He recalled that in the fifteenth century it became a practice of popes to shave a bald spot on their heads. They adopted the skull cap to keep the bald spot warm. Today popes do not necessarily wear the bald spot. But the skull cap is there all the same.) Today a state governor represents the will of the whole people demonstrably more fully than the state legislature, yet he is still treated as though he were promoting the schemes of George III.

All sorts of theory and doctrine have been invented to account for this phenomenon. Many American commentators find it almost irresistible to suggest that Montesquieu's propositions in *The Spirit of the Laws* provided the ideas for the separation of powers found in the state governments, including the separation—and hostility—of legislature and executive. "It seems more fitting, however, to regard Montesquieu's doctrines as a confirmation of something in which Americans had been conditioned for a century or more," says *The American Constitution*. "Long before Montesquieu they had become convinced of the desirability of a legislature removed from and independent of executive controls."

In many states the fear of executive power is reflected in the fact that governors are prohibited from succeeding themselves. In constitutions written largely by politicians with a legislative state of mind, governors are limited to one term. It is quite common to hear this limitation defended as a method of preventing governors from establishing political "machines." Anyone familiar with political lore in this country will recognize this reason as one commonly advanced. Yet it must seem utterly without validity to the observer who has examined the nature of political machines. Though Huey Long's was short lived, it was easily the mightiest in terms of raw power ever put together in this country, and of course a Louisiana governor cannot succeed himself. Virginia's governor cannot succeed himself, and yet Harry Byrd's machine has been not only among the most powerful but easily was the most enduring in America. In California, where succession is possible, nobody has been able to put together a really dependable machine since the railroads did it, and in New York, where succession is also allowed, almost everybody has a machine but the governor. At the end of fully six terms as governor of Michigan, G. Mennen Williams had not managed to put together a machine potent enough to get his legislature to enact an appropriations bill in time to pay state employes their salaries. These facts of history should be enough to dispel the notion that the often expressed fears are in fact the reasons behind the separations of powers and the legislative hostility to the executive.

As an instrument of a commercial constituency the role of the state legislature predated all the democratic impulses that eventually emerged. One may wonder whether later states should have escaped the implications of this. However, one discovers that in the later states, as they were admitted to the union, the commercial constituency and the actual governing groups were not merely close but were often synonymous. For just two examples, it is historic truism that the Wyoming Stock Growers Association was the de facto government of that territory and simply implanted itself constitutionally at statehood; similarly it is a historic truism that the mining interests of Montana, primarily Anaconda, could scarcely be separated from the state government when that great western democracy was founded. In their actual legislative forms the new states simply adopted and absorbed what had developed through tradition and custom among the others. Their differences were trivial, their likenesses substantial.

Historians and politicians are often enthusiastic about the rapid spread of democratic practices beginnning with the Jacksonian era. This enthusiasm does no harm. Yet, one should note that during the time of this rapid awakening— as both earlier and later—the state legislature was a resistive force. It *promoted* the advance of the democratic impulse only in a negative way: quite simply, the people began to hold the state legislatures in contempt and think of turning to the federal government. "The extravagant state banking law and internal improvement schemes of the generation after 1815 led to a growing popular distrust of the integrity and capacity of state legislators, a distrust greatly increased after the financial collapse of many of the states following the Panic of 1837." *The American Constitution* again. While the distrust brought agitation for greater popular control, and while the state legislatures began to respond by broadening suffrage, it is equally true that the legislative heart was not in it. "Reaction against manhood suffrage soon set in," says Bromage in *State Government and Administration.* "Connecticut and Massachusetts in 1855 and 1857 hastily threw up literacy tests as a barrier against the unlettered immigrants. Thereby they set an example which was not lost on the South in the years when Negro suffrage was an acute issue."

We turn to these earlier years for only one reason, seeking clues to the institutional character of the state legislature, not to mull over history for its own sake, nor to moralize about its directions and trends. Historians often treat theories and doctrines pretty much as though they were part of the reality of the times. A method of observation more elementary will serve the purpose here, which is to focus on what state government was actually doing. It is always necessary to peel back the doctrine and theory that sprang from what they were doing.

Take, for instance, a case that is accorded an important place in every history book and text on constitutional law. The case is styled Fletcher v. Peck. The U.S. Supreme Court handed down its decision in this matter in 1810. The case came out of Georgia and involved a land deal between the state and several private land companies. In 1795 the Georgia legislature granted the land, a subsequent legislature revoked the grant, and the long litigation was set in motion. Out of the Supreme Court's decision came a great body of elaborate doctrine. Because the court held that the contract made in the first instance by the Georgia legislature would have to prevail, the decision was of importance in building up legal theories about the nature of contracts between states and private individuals. Because the U.S. court ruled that Georgia could not revoke the deal made earlier, the spinners of doctrine took this to mean a variety of things about the nature of state "sovereignty." All this political and legal theory is fascinating. None of it, however, tells us anything about the behavior of the Georgia legislature.

What instructs us on that score is the knowledge that the Georgia legislature in 1795 was bribed, almost down to the last man, by a group of speculators served by a U.S. senator to grant for a price of $500,000 a tract of land that totaled some 50 million acres. It spanned—to suggest the size of it—all the present state of Mississippi and half of Alabama. These facts, and not the theory that was subsequently spun out of them by lawyers and political philosophers, suggest the propensities, attitudes and capabilities of the Georgia legislature. When the facts of the original grant became generally known in Georgia, the state legislature revoked the deal and ceremonially burned all the records pertaining to it in bonfires in front of the state capitol. From the inspirational words of Georgia orators at the time it is clear that the legislature—or many in it—believed that the incineration of the records actually caused the prior act of the legislature to cease to exist—a proposition that readers of Orwell's *1984* may regard as strikingly premature.

It is perhaps possible to draw moral lessons from this episode, known as the Yazoo Land Fraud. But moralistic preachments do not tend to reveal any more about the actual behavior of the state legislature than do legalistic doctrines. What became clear in the Yazoo Land Fraud was the readiness of the legislature to dispose of the public domain in a certain way. It was perfectly willing to place the people's property into the ownership of private speculators at only a nominal, negligible price. In this attitude the Georgia legislature was not breaking from its own traditions but simply extending them. The customs and the state of mind that played upon the state legislature had stemmed from its colonial years just as had its visible forms. Both as a proprietary colony and later as a royal colony Georgia was primarily a commercial venture. The fact that it never became a profitable one did not make the commercial tradition prevail less upon the governing body.

By contesting the efforts of the Yazoo land grantees, the speculators, to cinch their possession of the land, the Georgia legislature was not repudiating the basic idea of the deal at all. It was only repudiating the well-publicized briberies, a gesture as understandable by politicians then as by politicians today in a time of professional public relations. The legislature was concerned about its image, not about the idea of disposing of the public domain in such a manner. That idea was already firmly fixed in the institutionalized mentality of the American legislature.

It is fair to inquire whether it was an attitude generally among state legislatures. It is fair to answer that it was. The Yazoo land grant (Yazoo was the name of a river) differed from thousands of others only in that certain acts of bribery became publicized and the size of the grant seemed to capture the imagination. Historians generally take the view that if a certain amount of abandon had not obtained in the disposition of public lands the development of the country would have been retarded. This may be.

Knowledge of this legislative attitude, however, is useful in understanding the behavior of the modern state legislature no less than the old. A certain legislative attitude toward the public domain remains a constant today, as any person who studies the disposal of public land and properties will vouch. Conservationists find the attitude impenetrable and inexplicable. That is only because the roots of it lie so deep. This attitude prevails so much, however, that the instances in which legislatures manage to overcome it are anomalous. For the most part conservationists despair at their inability to get legislatures to understand what is meant by conservation. History books ordinarily skim over all this in favor of expounding the doctrine and theory that surround Yazoo Land Fraud.

Another famous Supreme Court case that makes all the textbooks is Gibbons v. Ogden. In 1824, the U.S. Supreme Court handed down this decision from which all manner of legal and political doctrine was to be spun. The decision related to the federal government's power to control commerce. The court held it to be complete. And besides issuing this considerable chunk of law and theory, John Marshall appended one of his gratuitous commentaries, one that is pertinent here.

"Powerful and ingenious minds," said Marshall, "taking, as postulates, that the powers expressly granted to the government of the Union are to be contracted, by construction, into the narrowest possible compass, and that the original powers of the States are retained, if any possible construction will retain them, may, by a course of well digested, but refined and metaphysical reasoning, founded on these premises, explain away the constitution of our country, and leave it a magnificent structure indeed, to look at, but totally unfit for use."

In other words, Marshall thought the government was the instrument of the people, and since the people reign supreme they can do what they damn please through their government. If they can't, to hell with it.

What is further pertinent here, beyond the theory and doctrine, is the behavior behind the case. It came out of New York. The state legislature had granted an exclusive monopolistic franchise to one company for the operation of steamboats on the waters of the state. In 1808 the legislature granted the monopoly to Robert Fulton and Robert Livingstone. They sublet, so to speak, certain rights on the Hudson River between New York and New Jersey to Aaron Ogden. He was hauled into court by Thomas Gibbons, who claimed a right to ply the Hudson under a license obtained under the federal coasting act. Marshall's opinion asserting the superior right of the federal government to control commerce was of great import forever. It was of particular interest at the time because so many state legislatures were setting up the same kind of monopolistic deals—which is the point of behavior to be observed.

In this era, supposedly, rugged individualism was aborning in America. Yet, we find in the state legislature a mentality that was hospitable to this kind of cozy arrangement with private corporations. We find them here employing the force of the law not only to protect selected corporations from competition but, once again, to place the disposal of the public domain into private hands. There was a further willingness on the part of state legislatures to conduct retaliatory actions on behalf of their chosen monopolists against other legislatures doing the same thing elsewhere. That fact at least reveals the extent of the state commitment to their monopolists.

Historians have provided no general evidence to suggest that corporations subsequently advancing upon the nation's legislatures to obtain favors ever found those bodies sitting in rapt contemplation of the public interest. By the age of the Robber Barons, when Commodore Vanderbilt and Daniel Drew were battling for control of the Erie Railroad through the New York legislature, the only suspense at Albany was over whether Vanderbilt or Drew would win the auction. They didn't buy legislators like bags of potatoes —they shuffled them back and forth like poker chips.

The Dartmouth College case of 1819 was uncomplicated. It should be discussed briefly as early evidence of a legislative tendency that manifests itself from time to time in practically every state. The New Hampshire legislature, very simply, wanted to take over Dartmouth College, because the governor, and obviously the legislature, did not like the way it was being run. George III had granted the charter creating Dartmouth College in 1769, and it was being operated under that charter in 1816 by a board of trustees dominated by federalists. The Republican governor and his Republican legislature felt that a charter less congenial to "monarchy" and more amenable to "free government" would be desirable. They passed a law to transfer control of the college out of the hands of trustees and into a board of overseers named by the governor. The trustees went to court, lost in the state judiciary, but won in the Supreme Court. It held that the old royal charter amounted to a contract protected by the Constitution. This doctrine— which astounded lawyers at the time, it being the first time a charter had been construed as a contract and so protected —need not conceal the aspect of legislative behavior that is to be observed, namely, the impulse to intrude with the instruments of law and politics upon the operations of institutions of higher learning.

Only the antiquity of this trait is illustrated by the Dartmouth College case. The fact that the Supreme Court ultimately thwarted the legislature and the governor is beside the point here. The peculiar attitude of legislatures toward colleges and universities, public and private, is seemingly an unchanging characteristic. Through the 1950s and early 1960s the Florida legislature endlessly harassed the state's universities through investigations. Other instances have been cited earlier. The truth is that the history of nearly every state college is a history of resisting political tampering from the state capitol. Examples from many years and states proliferate. There is the case of one of the earliest of the western universities, "Catholepistemiead or University of Michigania," founded as a secondary school, rechartered in 1837 as a state university and allotted proceeds from the territorial land reserves. *Growth of the Republic* cites its history briefly: "As in other Western states, so much of this land was lost by squatters' claims and legislative chicanery that tuition fees had to be charged in the early days, and state appropriations sought later. The University was governed by a Board of Regents, nominated by the Governor of Michigan, with full powers to dictate courses, prescribe textbooks, hire and fire professors; powers which they delighted to exercise, and not notably to the advancement of learning—the first president who endeavored to establish professional schools and to emulate the standards of a German university was dismissed by the regents."

In the 1840s the Massachusetts legislature criticized Harvard for failing to make young men into "better farmers, mechanics, or merchants."

In 1965 the North Carolina legislature enacted a law to protect the state universities from subversive speakers.

Examples abound. The legislative mind is not attuned to freedom.

The value of inspecting early displays of legislative character is that it tends to free us from disconcerting emotions. Knowledge of the antiquity of legislative traits leads us to a clearer perspective. Much of the dismay, perplexity and astonishment that occurs among Americans who actually observe the state legislature results not from unusual legislative behavior—but because of the innocence of the observer.

The innocent reacts like a child who is discovering for the first time that man is a belligerent creature. It takes the child years to learn that this is simply a condition of man. Once he learns this he can drop his perplexion and astonishment and begin observing man's actual traits of behavior toward the end of developing a catalogue of the various ways in which man's belligerence is displayed and under what conditions. He is in a position to learn some useful things by observing man's behavior instead of reacting to it.

What has happened at this point is simply that the child-adult has ceased to postulate the ideal, fictional man against whom he formerly measured observed traits. He has become free now to interest himself in the thing itself and develop observations of some predictive value. He sets out to discover the enduring traits and characteristics which, all put together, are what we know to be man, like it or not.

Much of the dismay that is expressed about the state legislature is the result of someone's postulating an ideal, fictional legislature. There seems to be a powerful temptation to establish such a postulate in all areas of life. The land abounds with marriages wrecked as the postulated ideal encounters reality, producing poignant anguish. The anguish experienced by the innocent upon first discovering the realities of the state legislature is only less poignant.

There is probably no point in guessing when the American people gave up, more or less, on the state legislature. Certainly a national attitude was dramatized when the country removed from the hands of the state legislatures the power to elect U.S. senators—a sign of popular revulsion at the way the state lawmakers had taken to marketing Senate seats wholesale. Perhaps the ultimate disenchantment came during the Depression when the state legislatures responded to anguished need by chanting little slogans—and doing nothing. In the recent era of wars, of course, the state has been absolutely irrelevant to national feeling. Nobody ever sold any World War II bonds by singing "God Bless Utah." Today state politicians boast of great state doings—but nobody who bothers to look forgets that these big outlays only amount to a belated attempt to catch up with long-neglected business. I hazard no guess on the time of the fall of the states in the esteem of the people. I daresay that Daniel Shays had no great regard for Massachusetts.

I daresay, too, that this country's feeling about the state legislature may be generally summed up as an amalgam of dismay, puzzlement, disappointment—the results of unfulfilled expectations.

The nation's steady growth into a national system suggests rather emphatically that the people have long since ceased to nurture those old expectations. Like the long-suffering wife of a habitually faithless husband, they hang onto the shadow of the old dream until the end, but also like the disappointed spouse they turn elsewhere for comfort and support. In the wretched Appalachians they sing "My Old Kentucky Home," but they know nobody but Washington is going to bail them out of misery.

I suggest that the people's expectations of the states always rested only upon a political mythology. There is nothing wrong with this. Our expectations of the national government also rest upon a mythology—but not *only* a mythology. The national government, if painfully and slowly sometimes, has steadily delivered on the hopes of the society for improvement. It has thus been in harmony with the mythology.

The state legislature, I suggest, has historically stood in profound conflict with its own mythology.

It has stood in profound conflict with the American

dream—to use the more sentimental expression that evokes our society's persistent ideals and desires.

The striking discrepancies between what the state legislature professes to be and what it is are numerous.

The gaps between what it purports to do and what it does are vast.

Occasionally one encounters legislators who are sensitive to this deep conflict. Still, it is far more usual to find legislators who seem to accept the image accorded them in the mythology. They believe, in short, what idealistic theoreticians have said about the state legislature and what it has said about itself.

Increasingly, however, even these believers—participants in the proliferating organizations seeking to improve the quality of legislatures—express bafflement over the legislature's sorry "image."

What these baffled students have not understood, and perhaps would not wish to believe, is that the people have a deep awareness that their deep-seated ideals and attitudes are too often at odds with those that the state legislature serves. It is not that the state legislature does not profess to be the very heartbeat of a democratic society; it is that it has persistently been in conflict with its own profession. And its actions have spoken more loudly indeed than its words.

It has professed to be democratic, yet it invariably submits to cliques and oligarchies.

It has professed to be republican, yet has massively subverted every notion of representative government.

It has professed to be the voice of the people, yet it has placed its powers at the disposal of a commercial constituency.

It has professed to be the defender of state sovereignty, yet has flaunted the state constitution whenever expediency so dictated.

It has professed to be the defender of the U.S. Constitution, yet has thwarted its spirit in the service of a gaggle of economic interests.

It has professed to be the champion of individual liberty, yet has left it to the courts to protect traditional rights. One more commonly finds the state legislature trying to devise ways to legalize peremptory search and seizure than to safeguard the citizen from police intrusions.

The state legislature has professed to believe that that government is best which is closest to the people. Meanwhile, it has clung tenaciously to the power that allows an individual lawmaker to dictate the salary of every local constable and the mileage reimbursement that a county supervisor may draw. It is patriotically outraged when Washington sends aid directly to the cities and patriotically parsimonious when the cities come to the state capitol for help. The state legislature in short has stood in fact for government closest to all the people except those who live in villages, towns, cities, sewer districts, recreation districts, zoning districts, water districts, judicial circuits, counties—and states.

Likewise, the state legislature purports to stand as the last surviving bastion of free enterprise and laissez faire and competitive business and all the other get-up-and-go, nose-to-the-grindstone, survival-of-the-fittest, may-the-best-man-win traditions of the unregulated capitalistic mythology. But it has distinguished itself by fixing liquor prices, dictating the language to be used in real estate ads, establishing utility monopolies and refusing to supervise them, compelling barbers to throw away neck dusters, legislating the size of sheets a hotel must use, erecting interstate barriers in used-car commerce, prescribing the size of crabs that fishermen may sell and the shape of boxes farmers may pack asparagus in—all the while aiding and abetting the closed-shop tendencies of lawyers, doctors, engineers, chiropodists, beauticians and masseurs.

A priest in as deep a conflict as this with the myths and creeds of his church would probably go to pieces, turn to drink, flee to Mexico and shack up with a voluptuous female innkeeper just as Tennessee Williams suggested in the *Night of the Iguana*. To reverse the thought, a priest who fled to

232

Mexico and turned into an alcoholic voluptuary would hardly be in deeper conflict with his church's mythology that the state legislature is with its own.

Under the weight of such psychic stress a certain amount of curious behavior is to be expected.

I seriously doubt that the malaise will prove fatal. Hence I terminate these notes and comments without joining those who prophesy the end of the states.

As a source of humor alone the state legislature fulfills a valid social function, and as custodians of the obsolete and passé it has proved itself indispensable.

I suspect the state and its legislature will be with us for some time.

Certainly it is a spectacle for which the American observer should give thanks. The welling emotions experienced by those privileged to watch have been handsomely described by Albert J. Abrams, the secretary of the New York state senate. "In the fifty states," Abrams wrote, "ninety-nine men, my colleague-secretaries, stand on the dais of their respective chambers and look out upon the great, on-going experiment in representative government. *Here before their eyes is what men have died for on many a bloody battlefield.*" (Emphasis added.)

BETHANY

DISCARD